Me

and My

Shadow

Ray Matthews

PNEUMA SPRINGS PUBLISHING UK

First Published in 2012 by:
Pneuma Springs Publishing

Pneuma Springs

British Library Cataloguing in Publication Data

Matthews, Ray.
  Me and my shadow.
  1. Matthews, Ray. 2. Long distance runners--Great
  Britain--Biography.
  I. Title
  746.4'2'092-dc23

ISBN-13: 9781907728358

Pneuma Springs Publishing
A Subsidiary of Pneuma Springs Ltd.
7 Groveherst Road, Dartford Kent, DA1 5JD.
E: admin@pneumasprings.co.uk
W: www.pneumasprings.co.uk

Book reviews

It has been a real pleasure to read "Me and My Shadow". It is an inspirational book where the author has bravely shared so much of himself and his journey. I am intrigued by extraordinary stories of determination, and achievement, whereby adversity is overcome and goals are reached. This book is a perfect example of this. The author takes you on a journey and leaves you wanting more, always the mark of a great book.

Marina Tune
Child and Adolescent Psychotherapist

— — — — — — — — —

I am so glad that I took the time to read "Me and My Shadow". Once I began reading I did not want to put the book down, neither did I want it to end.

The author Ray Matthews takes you on a journey throughout his life, and as a reader, you feel that you are part of that journey.

I felt like I was the "shadow" referred to in the title. The descriptive writing and storytelling painted such an imaginative picture that I felt I was right there besides him, like I was Ray's shadow. I felt the physical and emotional pain Ray had experienced, and I felt the overwhelming joy of knowing that he had just taken part in something truly amazing.

The book is such an inspirational read and anyone who is seeking a dream and wanting to take on the impossible should read this book. I would like to thank Ray for sharing his journey and letting me be part of it through his beautiful writing.

Helen Woodburn-Moran

— — — — — — — — —

Ray writes with a passion that reflects his fervor for life. His heartfelt desire is to be all he can be, to collect and soak in every experience, and to grow as a human being and as an athlete. As you read you would almost feel you are there with Ray as a young lad, as he takes steps that help him discover his most important mentors who lead him to make the hardest decisions that made the biggest differences in his life as an athlete, family man, and business man. If you have the burning desire to live your life on your terms, then Ray's book is a must read. Ray is living the ideal life; to be content with what he has achieved, and be ambitious for more. Don't wait too long to write your next book Ray.

David Greenfield
Gym buddy and Life Coach

Throughout a lifetime, everyone has the opportunity to meet truly exceptional people. I have. But only very few times have I met someone who inspires, the way Ray does. He turns concepts around, demonstrating the relativity of the "biological clock" and what can and cannot be achieved by having the right mindset.

Who decides what the right age is to achieve your dreams.

How many times does society impose the things we should or should not do, and what is seen as "reasonable", and what is expected of us. There is timing for everything. Ray demonstrates that destiny is in your hands, and not in the hands of what society expects of us.

Even today, practicing for sport, or in my work, or family environment, I still think back to the phrases, or moments I was able to share with this incredible man, and friend.

Ray truly is, an inspirational story himself.

Patrick De Jong
Desert runner and Friend

———————

There are many words to describe how I feel after reading Me and My Shadow, intrigued, shocked, emotional, inspired, but most of all proud. I am proud that I know Ray, and honoured that he turns up week in week out to my fitness classes. For the advice, his knowledge, and the time he has given me over the past few years.

His enthusiasm to his sport is mind blowing, and whatever Ray puts his mind to, he achieves it with flying colours. From being this cocky ginger haired, Yorkshire lad who just wanted to "have a go at boxing", to his recent 100km Sahara Desert race, Ray has, and always gives 110%. He is an absolute credit to anyone who knows him.

This book gives a great insight into the "down to earth" Ray (we thought we knew)! Some of the stories are very funny, as well as inspirational. An immensely gripping read, a must buy. Thanks for everything Ray.

Fiona Burkinshaw
Personal Trainer and fitness coach

Dedication

I would like to dedicate this book, and pay my personal tribute, to the memory of an exceptional Athlete, Coach, and founder of the International Rowbotham Round Rotherham annual foot race, Ralph Rowbotham.

Ralph who sadly passed away on the 16th of September 2010 will be sadly missed by everyone whose life he touched. His legacy will live on, as his event continues to grow from strength to strength.

Thanks and Acknowledgments

To my granddaughter Holly, for providing me with the perfect feelings and frame of mind at the start of my 100 mile journey. Everyone should at sometime in their lives, feel as good as I did during our first six miles of this challenge. You helped to set the motivational and inspirational pendulum in motion. Thanks Holly.

— — — — — — — — —

To my family, friends and colleagues at the gym, who have provided the inspiration, and encouragement for the most daunting, and challenging task of all, writing this book.

— — — — — — — — —

A big thank you to Marina Tune, who first suggested that I had a story to tell, and encouraged me to physically sit still long enough to produce this account of some of the more interesting aspects of my life.

"You have a story to tell, and should write a book" has been a regular comment over the past couple of years. Well, here it is at last.

An introduction to my early life

I am Ray Matthews. Having reached the age of seventy, I am gratefully blessed with an abundance of good health, which is fuelled, and regularly topped up, by being able to exercise, and train to a fairly high standard. Over the past few years, retirement has given me the opportunity to fulfil some of the dreams, and ambitions that I was not able to take on whilst I was fully pre-occupied, running a business, and providing a living for my family.

Over the past couple of years I have been able to successfully complete a 100km race across the Sahara Desert and more recently taken on a very demanding 100 mile run around the circumference of Rotherham, South Yorkshire. But the very thought of writing a book; where to start with the story, and if I would ever be satisfied that it was good enough to let the public read the contents, has been an even greater challenge than any daunting task I have ever taken on in my life.

The story you are about to read is a small, but very significant part of my life, which I hope will inspire at least one person sufficiently enough to take on a challenge, and achieve a state of mental and physical satisfaction that they would only normally dream about. You can take control, and live your life purposefully, to your own making, and forge out your destiny, or you can stay with, or become part of the flow, and move aimlessly along with other people. It's your choice; dreams really can be made to come true.

I was born in Masbrough, Rotherham, South Yorkshire; it has to be said, at a time when a certain Mr Adolf Hitler was still throwing bombs at us. I am the eldest son of a family of four brothers, Alan, Peter and David. The age gap between us was not that significant, and as we boys grew to a more even size, the first up was usually the best dressed. Patches were stitched onto patches; Socks were darned over a jam jar bottom and cardboard usually ended up inside our shoes to provide something of a sole. It was a soggy experience when it rained. If I was to step on a coin in those days I could usually tell if it was heads or tails up, without looking down. But no 'we didn't live in a shoe box'. Ah ah!

For my Parents Howard and Constance it was a continual struggle, like most families I suppose, during, and for sometime after the war, bringing up a large family of boys. Unfortunately, to make matters worse, my dad had a seven year spell off work during my early years. He suffered from a severe injury to his back, which was caused by the lugging and delivering of huge sacks of coal around the local streets of Masbrough. He had sustained a slipped disc and ended up in traction at the Fullwood Annex hospital in Sheffield for over two months. He then spent more than two years in a full plaster cast jacket at home, which must have been so uncomfortable, and painful to say the least. We boys would spend many an hour scratching his back; using homemade flue brushes made from our discarded tooth brushes, which we would attached by string to sticks long enough to reach down the cavity.

Left to right- Peter, Ray, Mum, David, and Alan

I remember visiting my dad during one spell of treatment at the hospital in Fullwood, with my Mum. Travelling to the hospital took up most of the day, as we boarded the tram in Rotherham, slowly working our way to Sheffield, and then by bus up to the hospital on the outskirts of Sheffield. It was a bit of an adventure for me, travelling to Sheffield was like visiting another country. My Dad, who I hadn't seen for nearly two months was actually receiving treatment as we arrived, but because we had come all the way from Rotherham, we were allowed to visit him, and were taken down to a treatment room by one of the nurses. I distinctly remember the strong smell of disinfectant as we walked down the old green and cream tiled corridors, following this nurse through a maze of what seemed like never-ending tunnels, at more of a run than walk. I was definitely not prepared for the traumatic vision that met us as we entered this high ceiling treatment room, an image, which has remained with me all these years and still makes me sweat when I think about it. My dad was hanging almost naked, dangling from a strap around his neck, which was suspended from the ceiling of this cold and dismal looking room. I honestly thought they were hanging him. My mum almost collapsed to the floor as she witnessed the vision in front of her. They were stretching his back; my Mum was told, preparing him for his second plaster cast jacket, having removed the first one an hour before we had arrived. When they eventually cut this plaster support from him, the nurse found marbles, lost tooth brushes, and even a small toy car, which had gotten lost down the cavity. My Dad's injury created a huge financial problem for us all, being unable to work, and earn a living for our family, leaving my mum to provide, as she became the sole bread winner of the family.

Fortunately for us all, my mum had a great voice, which she used and which brought in enough money to provide the basics for us all, as she travelled around the area singing at the local affiliated workingmen's clubs. East Dene, Canklow, Brinsworth, Brown Street working men's club in Masbrough, and the Trades club, just off the Chantry Bridge in Rotherham were frequent venues for Mum, where she would perform Sunday dinner and evenings, sometimes during the week, and always having to travel by bus to the outlying areas which took forever, often not getting home before midnight. Whilst all this was going on, the responsibility for having to look after my three younger brothers was placed squarely on my shoulders whilst Mum was out working. Most weekends I would have to cook a full Sunday dinner for the family, even before I reached the age of ten. This could never happen in today's society, but for me, it was so natural and necessary then. There were no financial hand outs for us during this early part of my life, and the much used phrase of, 'We are going to end up in the workhouse' was a stark reality waiting to happen. Dodging the milkman, coalman, and rent man, on collection days was a way of life that I thought was just normal.

Looking back at the situation, during my early years, I had this feeling of being shackled to my younger brothers, having to be responsible, and take them with me wherever I went. It's easy to see why I had this rebellious streak in me. I needed my own space from time to time, and resented the responsibility placed upon me for keeping them amused, and safe. I would often sneak off, and disappear for hours exploring areas up past Thornhill School, on to James Street, and over the railway bridge, passing the noisy Heaton's foundry, where they made cast iron baths. The black dust would be billowing out from the open doors, and would cover the streets, making everything look dark grey and dingy around the area. Nearly every time I passed the foundry, heading up towards the Clough woods, there would be men with leather aprons, rolled up sleeves, and black faces, stood outside trying to get some fresh air into their lungs. Ironically they would all be smoking.

My usual destination, when I needed to be on my own was the Greasbrough dams, located west of Greasbrough, about seven miles away from my terraced house in Holland Place. In my early years I would become an explorer, running up and down the Indian warpath to Bassingthorpe and across the open fields to the dams. 'Is this where the distance running originated?' Could well be, as I recall being able to run effortless for long spells without feeling the fatigue that comes with age. This area drastically changed over the next few years, as house building work started, violating my direct route through the woods and open fields to the dams. Kimberworth Park soon became the largest housing estate in Europe, housing hundreds of families in such a short space of time. This also took away my chance of earning a bit of spending money, during the summer months, from the group of men who would turn up on a Sunday morning to gamble. They played Pitch and Toss in a natural concaved area to one side of the main path. Using three coins, which they would throw up spinning in the air, depending on the outcome of the settled coins, heads, or tails, and the bet placed on the outcome, would win or lose. I was paid a Bob, (an old shilling); to watch out, and warn them should we have a visit from the coppers, who sometimes raided the gambling ring. I would scrim up a tree close by, from where I could see for miles. I remember once spotting, and shouting" COPS"; the entire group disappeared, in every direction, leaving a good amount of money in the ring, which I had time to collect before making my way home, in the opposite direction to the cops. 'Good morning's work'.

The main area of my leisure time was spent right on my doorstep, Thornhill Rec (recreational field) a large open grass field, which stretched from Glasshouse Street at the bottom, up to Thornhill at the top, with Tenter Street running up one side and mainly Brown Street up the other. It's now a by-pass. This field catered for just about all the activities a young boy needed, from football, cricket, peggy, rounders, kite flying, sledging in the winter and just about any game you could mention, but not just for us boys. Sunday would see the turnout of the local men, who would make up a team to play us at football, or cricket. Their team changed frequently as they made their way down from Brown Street Workingmen's Club, and sometimes joined the game completely sozzled, which made great fun for us boys. Parents would often join in with our activities over the weekend. I have seen a game of cricket, played between two tin dustbins last for over sixteen hours, scores would reach the thousand. We would take it in turns to go home for food, and then back out as soon as possible to keep your team from loosing, "Happy days." It seemed that summers were always sunny, and extended by months as we experienced the Indian Summers, which often stretched on until the end of September.

We had a freedom that was taken for granted, without many of the fears of today's stressful problems. Amusing ourselves was easy during my childhood. If we were not out playing games, our time would be spent as a family in the kitchen, where Mum would be sowing, darning, or altering clothes to fit the next one down. We all sat around by the light of the glowing coal fire listening to radio programs, like Dick Barton Special Agent, Paul Temple, The Archers, Twenty Questions and Mrs Dales Diaries, always assuming of course that the large acid battery had been charged or the multitude of valves inside the old brown Bakelite radio was still working. Our vivid imaginations made these programs come alive, and were as exciting for us then, as today's computer games. We still hadn't had electricity installed into our terraced house in Holland Place.

Growing up, and taking responsibilities early on in my life, I believe, set the scene for my adult life. Commonsense and education in life was more important than academic qualifications for me. It was always assumed that I would become either a professional footballer or boxer. But isn't it strange how life provides twists and turns along the way to completely change the mapped out route into something completely different. I have made my decisions and choices at every crossroad along the way, and for better or worse with many years now under my belt; here I am telling you my story.

1
Let the journey begin

Holly and Ray

What makes anyone want to run 100 miles? This is a question that has been levelled at me more than any other, and certainly more times than I can remember over these past few weeks, since I was confident enough to make public that I would be attempting to complete the double fifty mile Robothams Round Rotherham event back to back. Well, I suppose the answer to that one would be better explained as we go along, but this is a self inflicted challenge for me, and without any other pressure, than a deep rooted need to satisfy a whim. 100 miles is a magical number, which I suppose few athletes would ever dream of attempting. But since I have never considered myself as being a proper athlete, and as it's also highly unlikely that I would ever win races that normal athletes under the age of eighty enter, this then is the sort of challenge that has provided me with enough focus and inspiration to become as good an athlete as I possibly can be. This sort of distance was not going to be taken on lightly, although there are many endurance athletes out there that would make this distance seem like a stroll in the park, and are performing these sorts of incredible distances on a regular basis, but I would not attempt to take on this challenge, at least without being as fit and mentally prepared as I could possibly be. The decision had to be left before announcing what I was about to attempt, and certainly not until I was confident that the physical training was over, and I was tapering down free from injury. A small niggle I could handle for the fifty mile event, but certainly not one hundred miles.

I just happen to have this positive mind set, and fortunately a strong enough body, like most endurance runners, to keep putting one foot in front of the other, more times than most other athletes. I have this need to answer my own question, how much further it is possible to push the limits of my mind and body. Will this distance give me the answers? Is there really a limit as to how far I can propel my body forward, over a relatively short period of time without a rest, and not only measured in miles, but also in effort? Age plays a massive part of the overall reason for putting myself through what is about to take place. I am running out of time, and fast;

I have had a pretty successful year in terms of running reasonably free of any major injuries. Having completed the100km Del Sahara Race, the London and Edinburgh marathons, together with a number of local and international shorter distance races, I figured that this year is probably about the best opportunity for me to attempt this great event.

I had set about my increased miles of training towards the end of June, but kept my intentions closely to myself for some time about attempting to take on this distance. Using local club races and together with the normal local training routes, I steadily built up my fitness levels. I had also spent many hours running sections of the Round Rotherham routes with a group of athletes from my local gym in Parkgate. Although, in reality, training for this sort of distance is a lottery anyway, because you could never put in seventy or eighty mile training runs on a Saturday morning for your long run, like you would do a twenty miler for your long run whilst training for a marathon. It really is a different animal, and the training for me, takes on a deeper look at my capabilities to recover quickly enough from one session, and then have the ability to be able to train hard again the following day without feeling fatigue, or experiencing muscle breakdown. It's a fine balance between getting it right, and picking up a severe injury, due to overtraining. Strength training is also as important to maintaining good core stability, posture, and strong bone structure, together with sufficient calorie intake to maintain the fuel requirements of the more demanding ultra running. It's a bonus for me understanding my own needs; after all I have had almost seventy years to get it right.

No sooner had I made my intentions public, and announced that I was definitely attempting this distance, it soon became evident to me that I had created another element that would be added into the melting pot.

The send off gang. Left to right - Caroline, Brian, Barbara and Alice. Holly, Ray, David, John, Pete and Ken

'Pressure'; Pressure was soon being asserted, coming in thick and fast from colleagues and fellow athletes. "No chance, not at your age" and "How many weeks is it going to take you" are some of the more printable comments. Most of these negative statements were quite predictable I suppose and understandable. But there were also good wishes and positive responses, which I had anticipated more of 'Oh ye of little faith'. During these early weeks there were times when the pressure within m*e* had to be dealt with. I had to battle with the pedestal I had put myself on, and the mental commitment to becoming successful in my attempt to become the first ever athlete to complete the double Fifty Mile, Round Rotherham event. Success will only ever come from paying the price. I am willing, and prepared to pay the price; physically and mentally. I know it's gonna hurt.

Have I got it right, is the big question right now well, we are shortly about to find out. It's a purely mental thing anyway. There comes a time when it's not just enough to think you're capable, proof is the provider of just about all the answers I need at this cross road in my life. I had declared some years ago that I would never make age an excuse for not doing anything. I don't have any limited believes, and have continued to take on bigger challenges year by year. Having decided to take on this challenge, I am now fully committed wholeheartedly and with a passion that will fuel my determination to succeed. I have created this positive momentum that I am confident enough to succeed against any odds that may come up against me. 'The older I become, the better I was'. What a true saying.

I felt the best option was to start the run by doing the double lap, and making the second fifty mile as part of the event proper, and getting away with the early 6 am starters on Saturday morning. The decision I then had to make was how long I would need to complete the first fifty miles through the night. Fortunately I am a local athlete, and actually live on the route and as this event was no stranger to me anyway, the chances of going wrong, or getting lost would be quite unlikely, or so I thought, 'But that's another story'. So I had decided to start my run on Friday the 15th October, late afternoon at 5 pm, giving me a good twelve hours to get back to the college, and the start of the 50 mile event proper.

All plans made, and on Friday the 15th October 2010, together with friends, and some of the Rotherham Harriers officials who were there to start me off from Manvers College at Wath, we stood on the start line ready to go. But before getting underway we observed a one minute's silence for Ralph Rowbotham. Ralph, the founder of this great event, who during the 1981 national steel strike, decided to occupy himself by creating this 50 mile trail race around the circumference of the Town of Rotherham. His patience and planning forged this great event, which I believe was originally intended as a relay race involving teams of eight runners, into a real classic. From those early formative years the Rowbotham Round Rotherham event has grown from strength to strength and become a true international race, not only as a relay race, but also as a world recognised endurance run, even providing qualifying points for one of the world's most demanding desert races on the planet, the Marathon du Sables.

Ralph had sadly passed away a few weeks ago whilst out riding his bike, one of his great loves. It is so ironic that I had decided to take on my challenge at this time. This run will now become my personnel tribute to Ralph, and I will dedicate this run and story to his memory.

I set off with my fifteen year old granddaughter Holly and friends; Elly, Fay, and her daughter Niamh, from the Manvers College at Wath-Upon-Dearne, and right on queue as if to reiterate that nothing was going to be easy with this challenge, the heavens opened and it started raining as we made our way down and out of the college grounds.

We were running at a good steady pace, after dropping off my friends who were running the first mile with me, which came up as we reached the newly built fire station. "Not far to go now;" was a comment shouted, together with good wishes, as Holly and I continued along the footpath towards the manmade lakes to our right, leaving the group behind. They said that the first mile is always the hardest; well, it should be a doddle from here on then. There's now only 99 miles to go, as we make steady progress along the canal towpath leaving Wath behind.

I couldn't help but admire the elegant easy running style of Holly as she paced out alongside me, even with the rucksack on her back full of her school books, and clothes, she was making it look so easy. What a great feeling, the joy of just being out together on this special and unforgettable day, bringing back memories of our training runs together of a couple of years ago. I could be forgiven, I am sure, for almost forgetting why I am here, and doing this challenge. Everyone should at sometime in their lives feel as good as I do right now.

By the time we hit Elsecar we are both drenched and covered in mud, laughing and joking as we climb up through the woods. I just hope she doesn't need her running shoes for school activities within the next few days; they are caked in mud and will need to have a thorough going over to get them into a reasonable state for use. I know what these young girls are like for clothes being just right, and in fashion. Maybe she could start a new trend in mud wear.

Our headlights were switched on and blazing a pathway in front of us, as we slowly lost the daylight, it was dark enough to make the lights worth using in the darkening canopy of the woods. It was still raining fairly heavy, and forming streams of water on the slippery paths. The rain water was converting into thick muddy pools as it made its own paths down towards the river below. We enjoyed one another's company, slipping and sliding about. I hoped she didn't end up slipping on her bum. The mud is over our running shoes now, as we climbed higher and out of the valley below. There had not been one complaint from Holly about the difficult running conditions as we scramble and slide about on the muddy paths up through the woods above Elsecar. This scene once again brought back great memories of one Saturday afternoon, whilst out training not too far from here, when she jumped both feet into a pool of muddy water on purpose, and drenched me from head to foot. I did manage to get her back whilst she wasn't looking later on. Both of us ended up getting a roasting for the state of our clothes. We looked as though we had been rolling around in a mud bath by the time we arrived home.

We were heading up to Wentworth Church, and about ten minutes overdue from my predicted time; Jacky, Holly's mum was there to meet us. It was the end of the run for Holly, I am so proud of her; she had done really well, and tackled the little over six demanding miles with ease. She is a very naturally talented young athlete.

"Aren't you going to be scared all on your own granddad? I don't want to leave you, are you sure you are going to be ok?" said Holly. It brought a lump to my throat. I assured Holly that I was going to be fine, and promised to be extra careful.

With a hug and a kiss I waved them off and set off up past the church, wondering if she would cop it from her mum with her muddy legs and feet in the car. I now felt suddenly on my own, and thinking, best get your head into gear now, as I turn to see them disappear down the road and out of sight. This is where it really started to get serious. Let's get on with it!

2
The desert beckons

Just over a year ago, I was travelling back on the plane with my wife Maureen and a group of Maltby Running Club members from a race in Prague, and reading a magazine that had been part of the race goody bag. Towards the back of the magazine, there was the usual number of event advertisements, highlighting and giving details of ultra races worldwide. One of these adverts in particular nearly jumped off the page at me. Every time I opened the magazine it would almost always be there without having to turn a page to find it. This event, the twelfth edition of the 100km Del Sahara race, a multi stage race to be held in the Sahara Desert, organised by the Italian company, Zitoway Sports and Adventure, held an almost magical spell, and fuelling my imagination, as I read, and re-read the advertisement .

The seeds were slowly being sown in my mind; and well before we landed I knew it would become inevitable that I would take up this challenge sooner or later. For a good few weeks after arriving home I did try to recruit friends and running mates to take up the challenge with me, but, "You must be bloody mad" was about the least offensive, and printable reply I got back. I had known from the onset that if I was to have a go at this one, I would be doing this event on my own. The magazine was put to one side after that first week, as we got on with organising, and planning our next events.

About six weeks or so later, in August 2009, I was on the start line of a race in Tywyn, Wales, running in an event called 'Racing the Train'. I was stood in the pack of athletes on the bridge, and waiting for the whistle to sound the start of the race, when I suddenly had this thought; 'you know what, anyone that's daft enough to race a train up the side of a Welsh mountain and back, has just got to be mental enough to have a go at racing across the Sahara desert.'

My mind was now definitely made up, and so a week later I had filled in, and submitted the application forms and received almost immediate confirmation that I was booked into the event, and had made the deadline as one of the hundred and fifty athletes.

I now needed to work out a serious training plan. But how does anyone train for a race in the desert, especially without the high temperatures, and living in Maltby South Yorkshire? That's a good question. Well, we certainly don't have much sand to run and train on, but at that time of year, November, December and January, we did have more than our fair share of MUD. Not exactly the same but it does have that same stamina building effect of sand running. It worked, but it does also have its down side, as it brings your relationship into a bit of a strain, arriving home most days with absolutely filthy, stinking running gear after training runs, with clothing almost impossible to get clean. Many a pair of socks didn't make it to the washing; instead they were diverted straight into the bin. You really do have to have a very understanding wife; I will always be grateful for Maureen's help and enthusiasm, she has always supported, and been there for me, even though she thinks I am mental, as I take on these 'scatterbrained challenges'. I also became a topic of conversation at my local gym, as I became known as that 'silly old bugger', who was regularly seen doing press-ups, squats, and running on the spot in the Sauna, So now you know why guys.

My training was going well over the coming months, reaching the peak of my fitness on target, and with about six weeks to go to the race I was as ready as I could be, feeling good and rearing to go, and just about ready to start tapering the training down, when I suddenly developed a very serious pain at the top of my hamstring just under my right buttock, which would kick in whenever I increased my speed, or put any extra effort into climbing hills. The pain was severe enough to leave me with no option but to seek professional advice. We fortunately have a very capable physiotherapist at my local gym. Phin Robinson, who has a room just off from the main studio. He found and diagnosed the problem within about ten minutes of excruciating prodding. It turns out that I have an almost unattached hamstring connection. Oh hell, that sounds terminal!

Treatment started in earnest, on what seemed to me to be a lost cause, and beyond all powers of treatment within the time span. The pain was taking my breath at times, especially climbing hills, or any type of speed sessions. It was 'A proper pain in the arse' as we say up north. There is a correct terminology for the treatment that Phin put me through on an almost daily routine to start with, but I prefer to describe the treatment ritual my way. Phin would stick two long needles into me, just under the right cheek of my bum, after digging around with the point of his elbow to warm up and agitate the area for five minutes or so. This would just about take me to a state of almost passing out. He would then attach two electric wires to the needles, they in turn were connected to a control box, which, when taken to the top setting, would produce a pulsating thump to my bum, rhythmically delivering excruciating pain and bouncing me up and down almost to the point of permanent levitation off the treatment couch. At times sweat would pour out of me like turning on a tap and I didn't scream once. Honest!

Thanks Phin. It worked. But I do think you have made me into a masochist since taking part in that concentrated treatment, as I am now able to stand more pain than I ever could before. Phin managed to treat me whilst at the same time I was able to carry on with light training, and not lose too much of my fitness level. A visit was also required to my local doctor to provide the necessary documentation as proof of my general health and fitness to satisfy the requirements of the race rules. I have a great relationship with my doctor, who probably thinks I am mental anyway, and was given a complete MOT check over, including setting me up with an appointment at Rotherham Hospital to take an E.C.G. test. I was given a print out of the results for my use, which showed that I was still alive, and complimented the file that I would need to take with me, to satisfy the rules and regulations of the race. I was as ready as I was going to be, and mentally I set myself a target, predicting a time of twelve hours to complete the event. Over the past few months, I had been reading books about Sahara Desert running in an attempt to understand what I would be confronted with, and the more I read, the more I felt that the conditions in the Sahara would provide me with one of the biggest challenges of my life to date.

3

There's light at the end of the tunnel

The rest of the first section of the inaugural lap went well and was quite uneventful, I managed to locate all the key turns off by the night's shadowy sky and aided where needed by my head torch. The climb up to Keppel's Column didn't seem to be quite as demanding this night as it usually was, as I set off up the hill, with my feet sinking into the saturated boggy terrain. The column itself, which is a 115 foot stone tower, built in the late 18th century to commemorate the acquittal at the court martial of Admiral Keppel, looked quite an imposing site in the moonlight. The shadow from the monument cast a long cloak like effect on the grassy field, making me feel very small and insignificant as I approached the housing estate, and on to the tarmac beyond the tower.

I soon passed what was to be the first checkpoint early the following morning, and then dropped down into the very dark woods with steep treacherous paths to the stream below. Up and over the very quiet main road, and then the long pull up to Hill Top at Kimberworth.

It was a bit tricky underfoot as I took the path down the steep embankment on to Medowbank Road, and then having to be even more careful, relying heavily on my head torch to pick out the potholes, as I made my way down the narrow uneven path towards, and then over the steel decked railway bridge reaching the towpath below. Soon I was heading out towards the Tinsley Viaduct and along the towpath of the Sheffield-- Rotherham canal which is very muddy and slippery. The rain had now stopped and the clear bright moon created a daylight effect, especially on the water.

This canal, but at a location slightly further down towards Rotherham, between the then Steel Peach and Tozer steelworks at Ickles, and the Don Forge at Rotherham, had triggered some great memories of my younger days, especially during our summer school holidays. We would spend hours swimming, and diving from the bridges into the water. We would build rafts from anything that would float, and propel ourselves up and down the canal like explorers on the Contiki Expedition. Being captain, dogs were allowed on board. I had a black and white collie named Billy at that time, which followed me everywhere. Bread and jam sandwiches with bottles of water would feed us until the end of the day, when the pangs of hunger would take over and remind us, it's time to go home. How did we ever survive from that much polluted canal water, back in those days, there was nothing alive in the water. We would see dead cats, dogs, and anything that had the misfortune to fall into that water, floating down past us. The only thing that moved in the canal was the occasional rat, and of course us Masbrough Street kids. Today the much less polluted canal is pretty clean, being full of wildlife and home to a large selection of fish.

I was still running fairly comfortable and feeling pretty good at this stage of the run. I could see the lit up viaduct ahead, as I left the towpath at Tinsley and on to the Tarmac at last. I had not had to use the head torch since leaving the railway bridge area, the moon had provided me with just about adequate lighting, but the well lit tarmac roads made a welcome change as I headed up Bawtry Road past the Pike and Herron pub.

I was very conscious about drinking regularly; I know the value of hydration. I had also been nibbling on dried fruits and nuts. It's so important to maintain the energy levels. I had estimated that I would need something like thirteen thousand calories, and about eight gallons of liquid, to keep me topped up, and provide me with enough fuel, and lowering the risk of running out of energy during this 100 mile run. There was so much going on in my mind at this time, wondering if I had got these facts correct; would I be able to maintain the energy, would I have the mental strength to deal with the fatigue that would inevitably affect me later on, and possibly well before the first fifty mile leg is completed. If I was wrong, chances are that the situation may become irreversible if I don't feel or recognise the symptoms' onset early enough to take evasive action. I had to be sensitive and diligent.

Much before I knew it I was making my way under the Parkway carriageway, down into Catcliffe, and across the closed off Orgreave road, turning left up the bank side heading out towards Treeton. The first time I felt that this distance was about to give me any problems, was when I felt a sharp burning sensation in my right heel, I realised that I had the start of a blister. The pain sort of crept up on me, it was more of an irritation at first, and then painful enough to let me know I had a problem. It was worrying because I had never been in this predicament before, and especially because it was so early into the run. This was definitely not what I needed at this stage. It had probably been caused by the rain and mud soaking into my socks, making the double skin section into a solid state, creating friction on my heel.

The Treeton Dyke lake, out to my right could now be seen clearly as I made my way down the path leading from behind the cricket club at Treeton. The sky was clear of clouds, giving the moon an almost daylight effect again, which is lighting up the water, and making the lake which covers a vast area, look much larger than I had imagined.

I was now running along at water level through the wooded path towards the Rother Valley Country Park, after negotiating the tricky loop back over the railway lines about a mile back. I felt more relaxed now, and less worried about taking a wrong turn, or path, anywhere ahead on this first lap of the run.

Running alongside the pay booth, and opposite the golf club, I approached the main road coming out of the Rother Valley Country Park, at this point a change of socks became a very important necessity, and I just had a sharp reminder to sort out the blister problem. It was a good time to have a short stop anyway, after the long drag out of the park. This road does go on a bit, it felt never ending tonight. A change of socks, an energy biscuit, and drink, really made me feel good and ready for the rest of the run until I reached Woodsetts where I would meet up with a good friend John, and have a short break.

Less than ten minutes later I was buzzed by what I suspected could only be an owl. I had heard the whoosh coming, and automatically ducked, feeling something touch my head as it came past, and then the whitish flash of the underside of the wings as it disappeared into the night, must be the headlight that attracted the bird. It is a bit unnerving being attacked by something you can't see coming. I had the headlight in my hand as I ran alongside the M1 motorway, and soon I was climbing up the hill, across the open ploughed field with Woodhall village just over the horizon. I was not going to outrun whatever was after me, but I felt better as I moved pretty sharpish up to the edge of Woodhall, turned right onto the village main road, and then turned left onto the public footpath after passing the house No 26 in the village.

I felt the nettles stinging my bare legs as I gingerly made my way between the houses, over the style and into the fields. It would be a much better journey for me the following day, after the hordes of athletes had trampled through this area and padded down these stinging monsters, my legs would itch for hours.

There were a few horses in the field; one laid directly on the path in front of me as I kept the white electrified tape to my right. The shadow cast made it look like a monster, my imagination was activated and going wild, but it was soon up and galloped away to my left, I think it must have been the light from my torch, because I was conscious of not making any noise and spooking the rest of the horses, as I continued, stumbling on my way down the very lumpy mud path, between the wooden telephone poles in the fields towards Harthill.

Harthill was now in view with the street lights illuminating the horizon. It seemed like no time at all before I climbed the steps out of the village and onto the paths up and over the fields with the newly erected wind turbines to my right. On one of my training runs I had been asked by one of the local walkers if I would sign a petition against erecting these wind turbines on the beautiful countryside skyline around Harthill. My signature didn't seem to have made much difference though.

The first of my food stash was up ahead, hidden behind a Hawthorne edge, just over the style leading to the path, which cuts diagonally across two fields. I had been out earlier during the late morning, around the course, placing Tupperware tubs with a variety of food for me to eat during the night, cutting out the need to carry too much weight on my back. I located the first of my energy food containers, containing two good sized crushed bananas, and laced with half a jar of honey. My mouth is watering as I prise off the lid ready to eat one of my favourite snacks, when I suddenly realized that there was quite a lot of activity inside the box, with loads of little black things moving about in the container. Oh no it was full of ants milling around. How did they get into that sealed container? Ah well, lucky I had my head torch on, otherwise it would have been meat with pudding ah ah! I now had to wait until Woodsetts.

It seemed that in no time at all I was heading out past Hill Top Farm, diagonally crossing the first field, still containing the potato crop, and skirted around the now very quiet Netherthorpe air field, with all the small planes parked up in uniform neat rows, just towards the tower and the buildings on the right.

4

My oasis in the desert

The 100km Del Sahara event started out to be something of a marathon. On Saturday the 6th of March just before midnight, Maureen dropped me off at Pond Street bus station in Sheffield, to catch an overnight National Express coach down to Heathrow airport for an early morning flight to Milan.

I had arranged to meet up with the other four British competitors, that were entered in the event and travelling out on the same flight, at about five thirty am in the airport lounge. Having made contact via E-mail some months before I felt that we had all become good friends without actually meeting. We had shared information about one another, and now for the first time these strangers were here in person, and not looking anything like I had imagined they would individually look like. Kenwynne, Hilary, Pat and William, came walking towards me as I made my way to check in. I just knew it was them walking towards me. I suppose the fact that there were four of them, was a good giveaway.

We all booked in at the check-in, securing seating for us all together, and then made our way to the restaurant for breakfast. I was starving. Whilst having breakfast together, we got to know each other better as we swapped information, and answered one another's questions.

We travelled out on the early morning flight to Milan. That was followed by a flight to Tunis after about four hours of waiting around the Italian airport food halls. Tunis airport, situated in the capitol of Tunisia, was our next meeting point for another group of about twenty five Italian athletes. We all acknowledge one another with nods and hi fives, as we congregated together in the departure lounge. This next flight would only contain the athletes that would be travelling out to the desert race, and gave me time to inspect the colourfully coordinated track suited Italian contingency. Wow, they looked like the entire Italian Olympic squad, with the black and red Mercedes sponsored kit they were all wearing. They were there to win at least the team event I had no doubt.

We eventually boarded our flight, scrambling up some ladder type steps, into what can only be described as a world war two prop plane. The one and only young lady cabin crew, who spoke perfect English, saw us to our seats, and after accepting a Worthers Original sweet from me, settled down, and strapped herself into a seat at the back of the pilot. I knew at that stage there was no chance of an in-flight film or meal, and definitely no chance of the duty free trolleys passing up and down the six inch wide isle. Looking around the cabin at my fellow passengers, nearly all of these long legged athletes were having trouble folding legs into shapes that would fit into a space which must have been designed for even smaller passengers than me. The flight took about two and a half hours as we made our way into the desert and Tozeur Airport.

I seemed to have spent a good deal of my time waiting at the airport carousels for my luggage to catch up and hanging around food halls, passing time on all that first day.

I was greeted, together with the other athletes at Tozeur Airport, by some of the Zitoway staff, and transported to our hotel for the night, arriving sometime well after midnight Monday 8th . We were allocated our rooms, and informed that we would be setting off, early for our Oasis camp site in the desert, which meant that I needed to be up for breakfast around 6am. I am still amazed that the alarm did its job and woke me from a much fatigued sleep. I made it for breakfast in somewhat of a daze and can't remember to this day what I had to eat.

We had made contact with Cliff, another of our British athletes, who had come through on an earlier flight, and together with the other Brits, we made our way to the waiting vehicles outside in the hotel car park. At around 7-30am our luggage was loaded on to the roofs of the waiting Toyotas by our allocated driver. Our leather coated driver was the size of a Sherman tank, and managed to load and tie off our luggage with amazing agility, never once did the lit cigarette leave his lips. The vehicle sank a couple of feet as he settled into his seat, which left little room behind him. Guess who ended up with that one? This seven seater seemed to be bursting at the seams as we all took our places for the onward journey into the desert. These vehicles were an alternate means of transport for our journey into the desert, which originally should have been by bus I was told.

We set off for the desert and the Oasis Ksar Ghilane, slotting about midway into the convoy of the thirty eight 4x4 vehicles. It looked quite an impressive sight, as all these vehicles headed out from the hotel slip road into the desert bound road. This journey took about four hours, along mile after mile of salt flats, and then through a barren desert landscape, on roads that didn't seem to have any particular destination. We made a short stop after about two hours at the side of a massive salt lake, which was being harvested for salt This road had been formed through what would have been a sea, some centuries ago. The heat of the day had been slowly rising; the vehicles air conditioning was working overtime, as the noise from the fan increased in an attempt to provide some relief from the outside temperature. We were soon passing through small villages with the local people lining the route watching our convoy of vehicles, as we interrupted their daily existence. Only a large herd of goats crossing our path slowed the convoy down, as we left the tarmac and got onto sand tracks heading out into the desert, up and over small dunes. It amazed me that we did eventually reach our oasis camp site out in the desert which seemed like a wilderness, without any of the vehicles turning over.

We were welcomed at the Oasis camp site Ksar Ghilane, by the full contingency of the Zitoway staff, and allocated our accommodations for the night. Canvas sheeted bungalows, set out in avenues of five rows of about twenty five of these so called 5 star dwellings. Each bungalow had a bit of canvas for the sides, and flaps for the doors, which fastened together with a bit of string. A tree trunk with branches held up the roof, and eight beds constructed at the base from two layers of breeze blocks with a mattress on top made up the residence for our gang. I reckon that the 5 star billing was because our beds were erected on two breeze blocks, making it more difficult for the creepy crawly things to actually jump up that high onto our beds. Nevertheless, this was home sweet home for eight of us for the night; two Italians, and six of us UK athletes, including our three female competitors.

The opening ceremony was conducted early in the afternoon, as we all sat around the picturesque oasis in the brilliant sunshine. The water was a sort of emerald green in colour. This colour is created by the living alga in the water. Palm trees provided some shade from the searing sun and surrounded the oasis which created this picture postcard like image I had seen in magazines. We had been asked not to bathe in the oasis, and didn't need to guess why.

The full contingency of athletes, sitting around the oasis, were introduced to the staff in Italian, which was then translated to English, followed by the highlighting of all the dos and don'ts of survival in the desert. We were then officially welcomed to the twelfth edition of the event by the race Organiser-Director, Adriano Zito, an x marathon-de-sable finisher, and a very experienced ultra runner himself.

Lunch was served later, about two thirty in the afternoon in the large Arabian style tent dining room, which was draped with colourful carpeted walls and floor. Rows of tables with benched seating either side, was set out and ready to cater for over one hundred and fifty starving athletes. Each table had an abundance of boxes of wine and water. The Italians, who greatly outnumbered the rest of us, were well and truly pleased with the wine. Lunch consisted of as much spaghetti, pasta, meatballs, and fresh bread rolls as you could eat. Fruit cake and fresh oranges, complimented the good quality meal and filled any last gap. If this was the standard of food and services we are going to get, then we are going to be well and truly looked after. We were certainly not going to be short of the right sort of energy food.

Later on that afternoon we were invited, tent by tent to attend the survival kit inspection. The mandatory race pack, for safety reasons, had to contain 1liter minimum of water, salt tablets, or concentrated electrolyte, a survival blanket, a whistle, a lighter, a mirror, and a chemical light. A hat, sun glasses, protective sun lotion, a small knife, needle and cotton, iodine, and Compeed blister plasters was also highly recommended. The scrutiny of my pack was carried out by a young Australian woman; who had just taken over from Carlos Garcia Prieto, the race course setter. Every piece was laid out on the table, thoroughly inspected and marked off the list with indelible ink. Towards the end of the inspection I was asked to blow my whistle. That's how keen the inspection was, nothing was missed. I put the whistle to my mouth and gave an almighty blow; the pea shot out and embedded itself in her hair. Not a sound from the whistle, only the laughter from everyone that had seen the episode...great start. Fortunately I had a spare in a pocket in my rucksack that provided the required sound. I didn't realise that real dried peas are used in this type of whistles, and obviously in my case had shrunk over the years that I had owned it. It was imperative that each runner had the required minimum survival kit, in case of emergency. Safety is of paramount importance in the desert.

Moving along down the tent and on to the race doctor, who occupied the next table in the line, I produced my medical certificates, and doctor's letter. The letter from my doctor, together with the E C G readout, stating that I was fit enough to take part in this ultra race across the desert, were all accepted, but who can ever read what any doctor writes down. So I suspect that it was really a document that says 'This man is crackers, and should be allowed to kill himself off in the desert' I can never work out how it is possible to state that anyone is actually fit enough to race in the desert. Heat and the harsh terrain make it so unpredictable, and can destroy a normally fit and healthy athlete in no time.

Finally I was issued with my race bib 'No 94'. Then standing there like a prisoner with my number held across my chest, the official mug shots were taken. I received a pat on the back from the race director, and good luck from the organisers, I am now officially part of the event. I was thinking at this time there is no going back now, what have I let myself in for this time, am I really fit enough to do this. There was a kind of nervousness that I hadn't felt for a long time in my stomach and chest. I think my heart rate just about rocketed from its normal low beat in anticipation of what was about to come.

Dinner was served about seven in the evening. As I joined the growing queue of athletes, the dining tent was filled with the sound of a variety of different languages, laughter and exaggerated voices seemed to explode as groups of excited athletes tell tales of their exploits during some race or other. I was seated close to a group of Italians, who were doing a good job of inviting, and involving me into the conversations that they were having about the London Marathon, which three of the group had completed a couple of years ago. They all spoke far better English than my feeble attempt at Italian. After another great meal of pasta, Bolognese, freshly baked bread rolls, an assortment of cakes and the sweetest fresh oranges I have ever tasted, and all swilled down with a box of red wine, it was time to say my farewells and walk back to our accommodations to prepare everything for the race tomorrow. It seemed like organized chaos in the tent as I arrived back, everyone had the same idea, looking around at the kit on everyone's beds, set out as though we were about to be inspected by the sergeant major. Eventual all the kit disappeared into rucksacks and calmness at last. Lying back, my eyes closed, wondering about tomorrow and what it would be like over the next few days.

Having taken care of washing, teeth cleaning, and hair brushing; for those who had hair; in what would be our last toilet block for some time to come. It was now time for an early night. The light disappears very fast in the desert, and everyone had the same idea as we settled down for the night, it was going to be a big day tomorrow. Soon all the talking had stopped, and silence fell around the site, it was also pitch black. Ear plugs would complete the silence for me, just in case we have any noisy sleepers in our party. I had been warned; I did sleep pretty well that night, and caught up with some much needed shut eye. It was going to be a big day tomorrow.

5
Must do better at school

I have often been asked, "What is the hardest thing I have ever done in my life?" This question has usually come after I have completed some long run or other, or a particularly tough training session at the gym. It's a question that has needed some thought over the years. But I do know the real answer, and it's probably what makes me tick, and is the main reason why I take part in, and sadistically enjoy the self inflicted punishment of endurance running today.

Many years ago, when I was a young boy, I can vividly remember, almost every evening, arriving home from school, with a black eye, bloodied nose, and usually torn clothes, sometimes all three; and all because I didn't know the meaning of diplomacy, or have the sense to back away from any argument, no matter how many of the opposition it involved, or the size of the challengers, I just couldn't back away; I suppose that's how I was made. I would then 'cop' it again from my mother when I arrived at home as I walked through the back door after school.

I had decided, after having to take on the Murphy twins, one afternoon whilst coming home from School, that it was time to do something about sorting myself out. I had realised that I needed to either, keep my mouth shut and back away, or learn how to take care of myself. I felt it would be easier to learn how to fight proper, and look after myself, rather than backing out or give way in any arguments.

I had made some enquires, and found out, that the Red Lion Pub, just off the centre of Rotherham's All Saints Square, had a boxing club at that time. I had decided that I would go down and give it a go without saying a word to anyone, not even my Mum and Dad or my brothers. It would have been a Tuesday or a Thursday evening, when for the first time, this Ginger haired, short trousered, eleven year old lad, opened the tap room door of the Red Lion pub at around six thirty in the evening.

With my heart pounding loud enough to deafen me, I walked through the noisy smoke filled tap room door and into what seemed to me like the lion's den.

It was unheard of in those days to see kids, or even woman for that matter, enter a pub on their own. There was only this one entrance, leaving me no option but to take the bull by the horns and walk in. I was determined to give the appearance that I was this tough guy and nothing bothered me. It seemed that everyone inside the packed out pub had stopped what they were doing, and from that very boisterous and noisy room, silence fell. It felt like everyone's eyes were upon me as the entire crowd turned to look me up and down. I remember gulping, my legs buckling, and the back of my throat seemed to close. The landlord who had spotted me, from behind the bar, pointed across to a door in the corner of the tap room that led to a flight of stairs. How did he know where I wanted to go? I wondered. Later I figured it out, I wasn't there for a pint, was I? I am just glad he hadn't ask me what I wanted, I know that I would not have been able to get a word out. I then had to walk across the bar, and again with all the eyes of the smiling, and laughing drinkers following me.

The thirteen steps to the door above were steep, and not very well lit. I remember reaching about half way up the stairs, my legs had turned to jelly, and I really did feel like turning round and leaving. I somehow made myself carry on to the top of the stairs, thinking 'what the hell, I am here now', and then knocked on the door. I could hear the sound of boxing activities inside, but no one answered. I really did feel like turning and running down the stairs and out of the building. 'The Hardest Thing I Have Ever Done in My Life' was to knock on that door again for the second time.

The door did opened this time, and a middle aged man, with a well worn face, bent nose and a cauliflower ear towered above me. "Na then young man what can we do for thee" he bellowed out at me. I will never forget these first words of greeting, from this man, Benny Kemp; who would change my life forever. "I wanna learn how ta box" I said, looking past him into the room of very experienced and professional looking men and boys. They were all going about their own training, skipping, sparring, shadow box, and one big strapping lad was knocking the hell out of a big punch bag in the back corner of the room. "Reyt" he said, "Tha had best cume in then so we can have a look at thy."

I followed this man over to the middle of the room; he sort of had his arm around my shoulders, in a reassuring way. But I really think he was making sure I didn't make a bolt for it, and disappear through the door, never to be seen again. A ring was set up at floor level towards the right hand side of the room, with bare hemp rope sticking through the mainly taped three roped arena. It was probably spattered dried blood marks which covered the canvas floor, and what looked like pillow cases in each of the four corners, made up the ring.

"Reyt lad, let's see what tha made on", he said, and then shouted one of the lads over, who had been skipping with a group towards the back of the gym. "This lad will feyt thy, so let's see how tha goes on wi him, and then weil let thy have a go wi a boxer," he said to me, as he started to put on, and then lace up a pair of, beat up and weathered brown leather boxing gloves that looked at least twenty five year old. The inside lining had bust open over the years and the horse hair was coming out as I struggle to get my fists into a comfortable position inside the gloves. I don't know what I had expected to happen on my first visit to a boxing gym; maybe sit and watch for a while, then possibly a bit of bag punching. But what was about to happen, and the speed of what was happening, was like a tornado that had a hold of me and was spinning me out of control, I think at this stage I was in a complete daze as we both walk over to get into the ring.

Now what could be difficult about getting into a ring you might think, I couldn't make my mind up whether I should roll in to the ring between the floor and the bottom rope, go between the middle two, or volt over the top. I decided between the top and middle rope was for me. My legs, I soon found out, were nowhere near long enough for this stupid choice. I nearly ended up with a high voice for the next month, as I trapped myself between the legs and the middle rope.

I stood facing my opponent, who seemed to have grown two feet, since getting into this ring that now suddenly felt as though it was a cage, and closing in fast with nowhere to go. 'Time' was shouted long before I was ready. I don't remember very much about the first thirty seconds or so, I was in another dazed world, but what I do remember is that I was suddenly being stopped because I was able to punch this lad with a sort of ease that I had dreamed of, and was well and truly dominating this fight. "Stop. Stop" I heard as the coach jumped into the ring to grab hold, and drag me off him.

"Reyt", he said to me, as he steered me into the far corner of the ring, "we now know tha can feyt", he said, and signals over this lanky lad who had been watching from the side with the rest of the room full of boxers. They had all stopped their own activities, and were now watching what had been going on. "Let's see how tha gets on wy this lad". "He's gunna box thy" he said. While one of the other men was gloving up my next sparring partner; Benny was offering me advice on how to deal with my next 'boxing' challenge. I honestly, really don't remember a single word he had said. I was somewhere in another world.

This time, facing me was an opponent who gave me the impression of being in complete charge of his ability to deal with whatever is thrown at him. He was also much taller than me, but skinnier, and completely different to my last fighting opponent. Just the way he stood, and the air of authority coming from him, gave me a sinking feeling. I knew this was going to be a much more demanding few minutes I feared, and it was probably going to hurt.

Time was called. With hands held high, like a professional boxer, and presenting no target at all, Cloggy Clarke, as I would get to know him, came swiftly at me, in and out, just hitting me where and when he wanted. He moved out of range with ease any time I went in to strike a blow. Within a minute of chasing him around the ring, and swinging my arms about like a maniac, I was completely knackered and gasping for breath. I was quickly running out of energy, and hardly able to deliver any worthwhile punch. I didn't know whether I was coming or going. All I could do was defend myself, as punches were coming at me from all directions. I did have the satisfaction of landing one good right hander on him, which stopped him coming forward, but only for a second or two. He was probably tiring himself out, with all the punching he was giving me. One round was more than enough for me with Cloggy, and as time was called, thankfully my first education in the art of BOXING had come to an end. We sort of shook hand in the centre of the ring. I think Cloggy had enjoyed himself; he had this sort of smiling smirk on his face, as he turned away to have his gloves removed. He had avenged his mate, and had given me a good pasting at the same time. I thought to myself, I am having you mate–sooner or later.

"Well done young-un" Benny said, as he steered me to the same corner of the ring, unlaced, and took off the old gloves, asking me to pack the horse hair back inside. "Reyt then", he said, patting me on my head, "A think we can mek sumatt on thy, if tha still wants to be a boxer."

I was instructed to come back to the gym the following week, with a rope for skipping, pumps, shorts, a vest, and a towel, I was also going to get a month free from paying subs. "Flipping-eck", I had not even thought about having to pay anything. That means I am going to have to tell my mum, and dad, and that was worrying me, because mum hates anything to do with fighting. I had been told off enough times about it, and now I was going to have to pay, to be taught how to do it proper. I didn't think that would go down well.

On my way back home, I remembered thinking about the evening's experience, determined, but wondered how best to mention it to my mum. The sooner the better I thought but I must get the timing right. If I came out with it when my dad was there, chances are, he would probably stick up for me, and come down on my side. I had got the hard part over with, hadn't I by turning up; anything else should be a doodle. I needn't have worried, both of them thought it was for the best, and agreed to give me half a crown to get some new black canvas pumps from Woolworths. They had figured that if I didn't keep going with the boxing, then the pumps would come in handy for school anyway, and I can use my school football shorts.

Going to bed that night, I couldn't sleep, I remembered, with the excitement of becoming a boxer, and of course I would become world champion at sometime in the future. Nothing would stop me now.

Over the next few weeks, the mundane hard work of training, and getting boxing fit, was just about all that took place for me. I lived and breathed boxing. Learning how to skip, which I had always thought was a girl's thing anyway, but had now become a big part of the nightly training routine. "Itle make thy light on thy feet and build up stamina," was the explanation for this exercise, which I learned to enjoy over the next few weeks, as I became more proficient.

Learning how to stand, move, punch correctly, and then blocking punches that was being thrown at me, was all starting to come easier as the weeks passed by. I was certainly feeling a lot more at home in the gym, and as I was now much fitter than I had ever been, I was feeling more confident week by week. Boxing fitness is a different kind of fitness to any other sport I have found over the years. The ritual of walking through the pub every Tuesday and Thursday evenings, and Saturday mornings, had also become a lot easier over the weeks. Now the landlord, and even the blokes sat around the tables and bar would shout, "hay-up Ray", as I passed through the tap room. I had become part of the gang, and felt right at home.

6

Will I become a big game hunter?

The moon was still providing a pretty good light as I crossed over the old stone canal bridge, creating a very special effect on the water at the very pretty hamlet of Turner Wood. This scene would make a great painting. I will have to do this run again, and bring the camera. Ah Ah Ah!

Whenever I reached this spot just over the bridge, it brought back memories of my time spent over the past few years of training up and down this section of the canal, from Worksop to Kiveton Park, and the friendship I had formed with one of the local residents who has the large garden to the left as you cross over the bridge. This pensioner has a laid back approach to life that very few people have. One Saturday afternoon whilst running up the towpath from Worksop, he invited me to come into one of his greenhouses, which was empty except for a pigeon. This bird had been seen floating down the canal, seemingly dead, and then he spotted some movement, at first he thought it was the fish nibbling at it. He scooped the bird out of the water, realising it was still alive, but barely. He had dried, and massaged the pigeon then wrapped it up in some old rags, leaving it in the greenhouse overnight where it was warm. Next morning, not really thinking the bird would be alive, he went into the greenhouse to find that the pigeon was moving about. After a few days of feeding and watering, the bird made a remarkable recovery, and then one afternoon after the pigeon had been fed; it did the most unusual thing. It flew, but in a circle, like following a Ferris wheel, with a diameter of about four feet. Round and round. It couldn't fly in a straight line. We christened the pigeon Loopy and joked about him having given the bird the kiss of life. We reckon that the poor thing was brain damaged from the time in the water. I called in a couple of times over the next few months to see the bird, but about two months later, a sparrow hawk had got him one afternoon as he left the safety of the greenhouse, and poor Loopy became part of the food chain. One of his feathers is stuck into the door frame for us to remember him by.

It was time to contact my friend John who would meet me in about fifteen to twenty minutes at Woodsetts. I was really looking forward to seeing him as I walked across the railway lines. The moon was shinning on the lines, which made them glisten and easy to trace, as they disappeared miles away into the distance. Over the style between the bushes, and small trees, turning right onto the bank side, making sure I didn't miss my footing and end up in the dike below the path. The stream is an offshoot from the canal. I left the farm to my right, headed up the narrow path to the woods and then down the steep, wide stony path towards the golf course.

Coming over and down the hill heading from the golf course into Woodsetts, I could see the hazard lights flashing from John's car, which was parked up just before the church. This guy is a saint. I was soon sitting in the passenger's seat, which had heat coming from it [heated seating], a flask of steaming hot coffee, a change of socks after taking care of the blister, and fresh trainers, I am feeling like a new man, John was also saying the right things, like I was about fifteen minutes ahead of my predicted time, which makes it just after midnight, and I looked like I had just come from a stroll in the park. Packing away some Christmas cake that John has brought with him, and spare blister plasters in my camelback, I felt anxious, after being sat for a few minutes, and was keen to get underway to test out my legs, to see how they would feel on the move again at this thirty or so mile stage.

Firbeck here I come, saying my goodbyes to John with thanks for all his help, I am on my way down the road heading towards Worksop, and then turning left onto the wide cinder track as I pass the last house on my left. Soon I am comfortably into my stride, and thankful that any concern about my legs was not really necessary.

The moon provided a pretty good light, so it was not really beneficial to use the head torch as I made my way past the fishing ponds. I suddenly became aware that I had a partner running with me; the moon had created my silhouette of about five foot as I changed direction after the ponds. My shadow, now seemingly ran in front of me, and brought back memories of a few months ago in the desert which created a sort of comfortable feeling that I was being watched over by a very familiar friend, who would guide me on to the end. I gingerly crossed the field which was usually an absolute mud bath, towards the Wallingwell house, which I believe was once a residence for nuns, some years ago. This field a few years ago, and after a particularly rainy period when the event was held during November, had given me, and a large number of the athletes, big problems. Having sort of waded knee deep through the mud, into what could best be described as quick sands towards the middle of the field. I began to run out of energy after losing a shoe in the knee deep mud, and had to make an about turn. After washing out the mud from my shoes and socks in the fishing lake, I continued on my way by skirting the field around the hedges and eventually out through the gate and back on track. Even in the summer months this field can be ankle deep in mud, and difficult to run across.

As I reached the lake at Langold I was conscious of a pair of eyes staring out from the edge of the woods towards my right. It was a fox. He was not going to move I felt, as I got closer he was standing his ground. These were his woods, and no mere mortal like me was going to pass. I slowed down to a walk and switched on my head torch, slowly directing the beam towards him, he looked about as large as a good size Alsatian dog, but with an enormous brush, "I am a runner" I said to him out loud, as if that could be the pass word. He stood still staring at me, and made no signs of moving. I was now less than fifteen feet from him, slowly walking forward, but towards the left of him. I stared to feel threatened, and even though I had never heard of a fox attacking a man I began to feel my heart thumping in my chest. At last as if fed up with this staring game he just slowly turned and walked off, back into the woods, turning back to check on my movements just before disappearing. Wow what a relief, I think if I hadn't kept on moving forward we would have been there all night staring at one another. I know that as time goes by, this story, for my great grand kids, will have grown out of all proportions, and instead of a fox, this animal would have been transformed into a ferocious Lion, or a Tiger, making me into something of a big game hero.

7
Sand blasted for fun

It's race day. Tuesday 9th March started with a 6am rise, I was just conscious of people stirring in the tent, and with the ear plugs in, the sound was strange and muffled, it was a new experience for me to wake up to a group of almost total strangers for the first time. I was sure it would become so natural as the week went on. We had plenty of time before breakfast was due to be served, and headed off to explore the site. There was a queue formed at the toilet block, and the waiting gave me time to talk to some of the other athletes alongside me. I soon struck up conversation with a tall Dutch runner called Patrick De Jong, who I found out later, was actually working, and living in Spain. He introduced me to his running mate, a Spaniard called Jose Luis Morillo.' They both spoke perfect English. Where else could you meet such a variety of people whilst waiting to wash and brush up? We met up again an hour later as though we were long lost buddies, queuing again, but this time for breakfast. I was now starving.

There was a good choice of food for breakfast and plenty of it. Leaving the dinning tent feeling good and more than satisfied with what I had eaten, a group of us walked over to our tent. I then spent some time preparing my rucksack again, double checking, and making sure I had all I needed for the race including the most important of all water. Lying flat out on the bed, trying to give the appearance of being totally relaxed and in control, until time for the start of the race, but my thoughts were in overdrive to be honest. I was wondering about the race and what it was about to throw up at me, with the realisation that in less than an hour, and for the first time in my life, I would become part of a group of athletes who would take on the Sahara Desert.

10-15 soon came round. I remember leaving the tent, and walking to the start line with some of the other competitors. There was this carnival type atmosphere around the camp; I could hear loud music being played. Three or four young men, sat on Arabian horses were being ridden in a sort of entertaining display, with the riders dressed in national costumes and performing great feats of horsemanship stunts. As we left the compound of the resort, the desert floor became a very different texture of soft sand, and getting deeper as we neared the start area. One of the local men was walking about with a young pure white camel, no bigger than a good sized dog, which followed him about as though they was attached. I realised that he was carrying a bottle of milk with a teat, and from time to time enticing the young animal along by showing the bottle.

I couldn't help but think as I made my way to the start line and looking around most of the runners looked younger than my own kids, and probably were. They were all talking in different languages, excited and nervous, but most of these guys looked, and gave the impression of being experienced ultra runners, and probably more than capable of coping with what was about to take place. They were certainly dressed for the occasion, in their very colourful licra tops, shorts, and scarves, but looks can be quite deceiving as I have found out over the years. Some of the most unlikely looking athletes have this amazing ability to surprise and run incredible distances.

The sky was cloudy and rather cool. Looking out into the desert where we were about to head, I could see large clouds in the distance. I remember thinking, this is perfect running weather for me, really, not very hot at all, and I could cope with this, I was feeling quite comfortable, but just slightly conscious of the heavy load I was carrying on my back.

Loud stirring music was being played "We Will Rock You", hammering out from two massive speakers which stood either side of the blow-up start structure. It's the real Mc Coy. Everyone was singing, and in English, probably nerves, but more than likely excitement of the challenge that was about to take place. What was it going to be like running on this sort of surface? The sand was getting softer, and I had visions of sinking into the sand, and slowly disappearing out of sight, never to been seen again. Well I was soon about to find out.

The countdown in Italian started, as we stood at the ready on the start line, and then finally the gun sounded. Off shot the lead runner into the waiting desert, and heading for the bright red flag in the distance. The field was soon spreading out with the faster runners leaving me, and creating this colourful snake like effect up ahead. Up and down, over the small dunes, getting used to running on this soft sand, and concentrating on getting my stride pattern right was my main priority at this stage of the race. Shorter than normal steps was working fine, it was certainly not like being on tarmac.

After a couple of miles I had settled into my pace, and was starting to leave runners behind me, feeling good I was at last on my way and into my 'zone'- average speed is king in ultra running. If in doubt, start very slow, and when all is well, slow down. Well that's my theory anyway, and it works pretty well for the more mature athlete who isn't chasing P-Bees. [Personal best]

More flags of a very bright orangey red were soon visible in the distance it was easy to navigate at this stage of the race; I could still see runners strung out on the horizon, like little matchstick figures, continually appearing and then disappearing in the distant dunes.

At about 5km into the race, I felt the first wind hit me head on. It sort of sneaked up on me, and as it hit me, it almost stopped me dead. That was quickly followed by the full force of the sand; it was like being shot blasted. Survival mode kicked in, covering up became priority number one, with goggles over my eyes, mouth and nose covered with the Buff I was wearing, [a licra tube which has about 10 different applications as headwear and scarf]. It felt like stinging pellets to my arms and legs, and I could taste the sand as it forced its way through the Buff cover into my mouth. Was I breathing too hard? Relax I thought. I have to control my breathing or I am heading for trouble. It's such a shock to the system and leaves you feeling very venerable and alone; because suddenly you can't see your hand in front of your face, and you question your senses and ability to navigate. Is this how I would feel if I was a blind person? "It's Bloody Scary" am I going to make it.

I had made a mental note of the next flags position and was confident that I was heading in the right direction, and leaning into the storm, when I stubbed and broke my big toe. The noise was like a twig snapping, which I heard above the howling wind. The pain was just sickening; I broke into a cold sweat, with the realisation of what had just happened. It was the sort of pain that when you were young, you would have wished your mum was there to kiss it better. Yes that sort of pain–I just knew it was broken.

I had also tumbled head over heels onto my back, and cutting my arm in the process. The blood trickling down my left arm was soon caked in a layer of sand which seemed to stop the flow after a while. Laying there cursing my stupidity for missing what was now a trail of bedrock that I was running on, instead of the soft sand of a few minutes ago. I sat up, and waited for the pain to subside. Looking round trying to find any sign of life or movement, there was just the sound of the howling wind, and peering through the blanket of almost solid sand with not much more than zero visibility. The sand was stinging the uncovered parts of my arms and legs. Now with my back to the storm I swilled out my mouth, which felt so dry and closing in with every breath I took. This gave me an almost panicky feeling of choking and a feeling that I had half of the desert inside me. The throbbing started again, I remember thinking, what will it be like, if I can't put any weight on my damaged foot. It was a daunting thought and one that I have never encountered before, I needed to blank out the pain and make tracks; I could be hours out here waiting for help. I got up putting my damaged foot to the ground, applying weight slowly. It wasn't too bad really, or was it. The pain, for some strange reason didn't feel that it belonged to me, and this gave me the strange sensation that everything was now taking place in slow-motion as I leaned forward into the storm testing the feeling of movement. I set of walking, and then running, but compensating, trying not to bend my big toe as I push off on the outside of my right foot, and headed off into the desert, but praying that I was heading in the right direction, looking out for flags, or any indication that I was on the right route. I had to concentrate on my new running style, otherwise I would get a severely painful reminder, every time I put my foot down wrong.

I remembered that the wind had been hitting me slightly to my left at the time of tumbling, which had left me a bit disorientated. Setting myself up, and with the wind again hitting my face to the left, I was now reasonably confident that I was heading in roughly the right direction, trying to pick out anything in front of me that would indicate the choice of direction was the right one, but seriously considering whether to stop, dig into the side of the dunes, and wait for the storm to subside.

The floor of the desert was now completely different, more of shale, and small rocks, than the deep sand I had been running on ten minutes ago, which was making it look more like a sort of road between dunes to my left, and complete wilderness to my right.

Sandstorms occur when the wind reaches around fifty miles per hour, and picks up lose sand and dust, often creating zero visibility. It's probably sensible to stop, and wait for instructions, as the disorientating effect could lead to running well off course. It has been recorded that an Italian runner ended up hundreds of miles off course and was found nine days later. It was a personal decision for me to take, and a bit unnerving at the time, but I trusted my sense of direction and felt confident enough that I had made the right decision to carry on

After a few minutes of running, well more like hobbling, I could make out a large dark shape to my left, and set into the side of a dune, it turned out to be a photographer, covered over, with what looked like a tent, with only the lens of the camera sticking out. He must have been sat there ages, waiting for runners to pass. I knew then I was heading in the right direction. It's a great feeling of relief, knowing you're not lost in this wilderness. I hope the cameraman is not claustrophobic in his little shelter.

Where the hell am I

I shortly came across a flag that had been flattened by the storm and blowing about on the desert floor, and tethered only by a rope to its base. The flag, which looked more like a sail, with the bright orange Zitoway emblem on both sides, made of nylon, and about seven feet in height when erected, was attached by a rope to the pole, which should be inserted about three feet deep, into a tube driven into the sand. I tried to erect the flag for the benefit of the runners coming at the back of me. It was proving extremely difficult because of the strong wind. I was now in danger of becoming airborne at any minute. I had visions of paragliding across the Sahara Desert, but in the wrong direction. Eventually I managed to erect the flag, and felt a sense of relief, and satisfaction, knowing that the runners behind me would have a target to aim for.

The sand was being blown off, what I later found out was an ancient nomadic trail. For most of the year it was deep in sand, but was now being exposed due to the wind, leaving a rocky bed, which I hadn't noticed. The storm lasted for the best part of two hours.

The first check point suddenly came into view out of the storm, with really sorry looking marshals covered in sand, and looking like zombies out of a horror film. As luck would have it, the race doctor had just arrived in his dune buggy. He inspected my toe, and confirmed what I already knew, that it was indeed broken. He told me that I would not be able to continue, and would have to pull out of the race. For the first time in my life, I had to either accept or fight against being seen as a casualty and a liability. Athletes are scrutinised as fit to carry on at these check points, and if in doubt they will hold you back until they feel you are in a fit state to carry on, or be pulled out of the race if deemed necessary

I was shell shocked, and felt like I had just been slapped across my face. There was no way that was going to happen. I couldn't comprehend what was being suggested. I was coping with the new style of running, and the pain wasn't that bad, I had enough to think about battling the storm which blanked out most of the pain. My insistence to carry on brought the race director to the check point, and after some time he agreed to let me carry on, only after promising to report daily to the first aid tent for checkups and treatment on my potentially serious toe.

Desert racers crave, and embrace the challenges of sweat, tears, bleeding feet and at times even hallucinations and best of all; we are even prepared to pay for the privilege. The epic achievement of just being able to finish is more than dreams are made of, and finish is what I intend to do. Any Liability out in the desert is a problem, and safety is paramount, I fully endorse and understood, but I knew that I would be able to cope with the problem, without becoming a burden to the Zitoway staff, or my fellow competitors.

I set off to complete the first leg of 25km, the adjustment I had made to my running stride was working, but still very painful, and how soon would it be before the real pain kicked in? I remember thinking this race really has just got tougher, but it will bring out the strength in me to overcome the feeling of being destroyed. Deep pain can cause you to struggle and plunge even the hardest of athletes into a pathetic tearful heap. I am here to explore the very seriously scary terrain, and landscapes of the Sahara desert, no matter what obstacles I am confronted with I intend to complete this race.

"I can't stop, I won't stop, I am a British athlete."

At last in the distance I could make out the growing outline of our camp, sat in a valley, looking storm battered and weary, but a very welcome sight nonetheless. As I arrived in the camp, the Berber tents were set out like the camp of a wagon train in the Wild West, in a circle and ready to repel the Indians. Looking up to where my tent would be located, we had been allocated tent No 25. As I walked up the line, I could see there was a gap after 24. I just knew that it would be my tent which was looking like a bomb had hit it. The Brit tent, as it was known, was flat on the floor, flapping about, and had been impossible to erect in the strong wind. It had also rained heavy, yes rain and my luggage was swimming in water. It gave me a feeling of being back at home in Maltby. The wind was still howling, and whipping through the site. You could make out the teams of covered up athletes, relentlessly working to keep their tents from being launched into the wilderness. Our tent was the only one on the site to be flat on the desert floor. Do you ever get the feeling that you're being tested to your physical and mental limits? It seemed to me that whatever could have gone wrong today; had.

But out of all the doom and gloom, and when you feel that everything is against you, the miracle of nature out there in the desert produced a special treat. With the rain came the sign of life, the wild and lifeless looking bushes on the outskirts of the camp, had suddenly blossomed into life with small pinkie white flowers, creating a colourful contrast to the bleakness of the barren desert.

Leaving the tent; a filthy blanket which smelt like the back end of a dromedary, stuck up on two dead tree branches, and tied down with bits of string, would be a far better description of our accommodation. I reported to the doctor for treatment on my now throbbing foot. The doctor sprayed my toe with a freeze spray, and bandaged it up; later that evening a pain killing injection was given after a great dinner with the rest of the runners. The weather was beginning to calm down now, allowing our tent to be erected. Peace at last. We would be able to sleep partially undercover tonight, although we had been making arrangements to spend the night inside the dining tent, if the weather had been too severe, making it unfit to risk further extreme weather conditions.

Later that evening as I lay in my sleeping bag, all tucked up and warm, I wondered how my keep fit class was doing, at the Wesley Centre in Maltby, where we hire out the hall on Monday, and Tuesday evenings for an hour with the routine I and my wife Maureen had worked out for them. I am a fitness instructor, and for the past three years have instructed a mixed class of mature students, performing a cardio, and strength training program with the emphasis on flexibility. We had decided on an aerobic workout for the gang, with music from Yazz and in particular Cotton-eyed Joe, whilst I was away in the desert, and as the time zones were exactly the same at this time of the year, there was no time difference between our locations, so at six thirty in the desert, it was six thirty in Maltby. Under the desert stars I slept like a baby all night, warm and comfortable.

Me and My *Shadow*

8
Learning about life at an early age

One evening after I had been training at the Red Lion Boxing Club for about a couple of months, Benny called me to one side, and asked me if I could come down to the gym half an hour before normal training time, for the next few weeks. Yes I could. I worked my socks off for this man, and did everything he asked me to do, without question. We had developed a comfortable relationship, and could talk to one another with ease.

I now realise that those next few weeks were to have a big impact on the rest of my life, as Benny set about teaching me, not only how to box, but also about ME. Our time together was spent not only on one to one tuition in boxing, but he also taught me about the values in my life, and how sport, but in particular boxing, would provide me with all the rules and values I would need for the rest of my life. Respect, discipline, determination, passion, and commitment, were all discussed during our half hour sessions, over the next couple of months. We would agree about the meanings of each one and he made sure I fully understood it before moving on to the next topic. What did I want out of my life, and how important was it for me to achieve what I wanted. This was an early question Benny had asked me one evening. I was told to go away, think about it, and give him the answer at a later date. I always thought, and was sure that he already knew the answer to that one.

My first outing in front of the public came during that summer. A traditional outdoor boxing exhibition had been arranged some months ago, and was due to take place the coming Saturday. The ring from upstairs in the gym was dismantled and re-erected in the square, outside the Red Lion pub, on the Saturday morning ready for the exhibition later that afternoon. The square is about eighty feet in length by about twenty five feet wide and surrounded by the rear entrances to the main shopping area of All Saints Square with an archway at one end, and an open entrance looking out to the side entrance to Woolworths at the other. I remember that a good few of the local drinkers from the pub helped to bring the ring down the stairs, and give a hand to erect a platform of about three feet high, and then they bolted the old ring on top. This gave the ring an elevated position in the square, and caused quite a lot of interest with the local shoppers, who often used the square as a shortcut to Woolworths and the Marks and Spencer's stores.

As if to mark the progress of my boxing career, for the first time ever, my name was printed on a glossy boxing programme that had been given to me that morning. There I was "Ray Matthews." It's a strange feeling seeing my name in print for the first time, and there was a bit of a write up about me underneath. I was billed as a promising junior boxer, weighing in at about six and a half stone wet through. That was definitely a guess, because I don't remember standing on any scales over the last twelve months. I would also be first to perform against some other young hopeful from the Phoenix Boxing club which was situated at Ickles, on Sheffield road just outside Rotherham,. I must have read that page a dozen times, making sure that my surname had been spelt correctly, with two Ts. The event was set to be staged for about twelve fights during the afternoon, and was due to start at one thirty. That Saturday I remember it was very warm, and there was no breeze in the sheltered enclosure of the Red Lion square.

The buzz of a fight show was always something very special, but especially for me being my first encounter with this sort of showbiz-like event. The opposing teams of boxers had started to arrive around midday, when all of a sudden there was a sort of quietness in the room, all eyes turned towards the entrance, as a group of really smart looking men and lads of all shapes and sizes walked through the door of the Red Lion pub. They were all dressed alike, with grey slacks, and black blazers with the Phoenix gold and red badge on the breast pocket. The Steel Peach and Tozer Boxing Club had arrived. They were intimidating. 'Professionals' that's all I could think, as I looked across the room, and spotted my opponent. I just knew it would be him. My stomach turned a summersault.

Benny came across to me, I know he could sense the fear I was going through. I was shaking and felt sick. He put his arm around my shoulders and started to explain what was about to happen. I was not to worry, everything was going to be fine, and I would be the first fighter on. That didn't help one bit. This show, Benny explained, was an exhibition only, there would be no winners or losers, and was put on to help all the boxers gain some valuable sparing experiences.

I was summoned to be seen by the fight doctor, who was set up in a small room off the main bar. What are they going to make me do next? I thought, as I was introduced to him. My name appeared on top of a list, together with my opponent's, who was standing at the back of me, sizing me up I felt. My first experience of going through a medical examination, from a fight doctor was worrying. I was thinking, would I be that bothered though, if he found something wrong with me so that I couldn't fight? Well it wasn't too bad really I suppose, as he checked my ears, eyes, mouth, hands, and then the dreaded hand down my shorts, and was told to cough." Why did they have to do that? I was then weighed and told to get ready. I still have no idea of how much I weighed for that first event.

The next thing I could see was Benny threading his way through the crowded tap room, and coming in my direction from across the bar, with what looked like a brand new pair of black boxing gloves in his hand, also a red waist band, and started to get me ready. The eight ounce gloves felt like lead as he started to lace them up, tucking the ends back down to stop them coming lose. I could smell the new leather from the gloves "Were gona be ok, so don't worry, just remember tha nar a boxer, and I am in thy corner so relax", he's telling me as he threw the towel around my shoulders and steered me out through the open pub doors towards the ring, and into the growing crowd. Everything was moving now at hundred miles an hour, and totally out of my control as we threaded our way through the large crowd of spectators. I was determined to make an elegant entry into the ring this time, as Benny walked up the steps before me to my corner - Red, followed by a very nervous, shaking and dry mouthed Ray. Benny was stood with his foot on the bottom rope, and pulling up on the middle one, inviting me to make my entry into the ring, a dignified one this time. How did he know what I was worrying about? There was this all knowing smile on his face, as if to let me know that he knows what I have been thinking about, and just nodded his head.

My opponent was already in the ring and dancing about in the opposite corner, like he knew what he was doing, as I made my first entry into the world of boxing. Benny was talking to me, and turned me round to face him, as someone announces my opponent, and then my name, I felt better for that, and his calming voice was doing the trick. All too soon the referee was calling us together in the middle of the ring, and told us what he would have from both of us. "I want a good clean fight, you will obey my instructions," he was telling us both "break when I tell you, and in the event of a knockdown you will to go to a neutral corner." He did seem to go on a bit, whilst all the time I was trying to size up my opponent, looking him up and down. He didn't make eye contact with me once and actually looked even more nervous than I felt as we turned away from one another, and walked back to our corners for last minute instructions.

Seconds Out; Round One; as a bell sounded from somewhere below me to my left. Now what? For a second or two I felt totally lost and exposed, trying to work out in my head how to proceed, It suddenly all came back, I had been instructed to keep my hands up, move around and jab, until I could work out where his weaknesses were. We both moved towards the centre of the ring, which I was determined to make mine at all cost. It's far easier to control the fight from the centre of the ring and make your opponent do all the hard work by having to move around you, and since I had learned how to control my temper, boxing had became much easier for me. I think I was now showing my metal because my opponent seemed to be backing away from me all the time, he gave little opposition, and had slow reactions to my faster straight left jabs, which were getting through at will during that first round. Sitting in my corner at the end of that first round, Benny went through the ritual of cooling me down, swinging the towel round to create a draught, and feeding water into my dry mouth. "Don't drink it" he said, "swill, and spit it out into the bucket. The bucket was offered up to me, from outside the left hand corner of the ring by a man who usually helped out at the gym. Benny at the same time giving me further instructions on what I should be trying out for the next one and a half minuets round, and at the time I was trying to making sure I didn't miss the bucket.

Round Two and Three flew by as I put into practice many of the moves, techniques, and punching combinations that I had been taught over the past few months. At one stage of the fight in the second round, I was held back by the referee, for a few seconds to allow my opponent to get his breath back. After all it was only an exhibition fight and I felt right at home and in control. Time was sounded at the end of the third round from this large bronze bell which stood on a table below the ring at the far side. Sat at this table where three official looking men in suits. I later found out that these men were officials from the Yorkshire branch of the Amateur Boxing Association, and there to oversee the event.

My first fight was over, and although I was not to be awarded a win or lose, deep down I knew that had this been a scoring tournament, I would have been the winner. I felt for the first time the incredible joy of being able to perform in front of a crowd. It felt as though I had been performing on a stage. The crowd, I realised where on my side and shouting my name. I was of course the lad from the local club. I must admit that I hadn't been aware of the noisy crowd during the fight, and hadn't heard a sound during any of the three rounds. "Well done young un, we would have won that if it had been a proper feyt" Benny said, lifting the middle rope for me once again to get out of the ring and down the steps, into the crowd who cleared a path for me back to the pub. Tables with rows of sandwiches, buns, pop, and beer for the big lads greeted me. Best thing about fighting first was you get the first choice of buns, before anyone else gets at them. I didn't get much chance of talking to Benny for the rest of the afternoon, as he took care of the rest of our club fighters. It was just a brilliant feeling to be part of all this activity as I watched the rest of my club mates going through the same stages of getting ready, and then performing in the ring as I had done earlier. For most of them it was nothing new, but for one or two, they seemed more nervous than I had been, which had made me feel better. I did enjoy being part of the team and felt a bit of a celebrity as complete stranger came across to me and wanted to shake my hand. By about five thirty the show was all over and the ring was dismantled again and taken back upstairs. "Well done young-un. Sithy Tuesday neet," said Benny, as we all started to leave the pub. I couldn't wait; as I ran all the way home to tell my mum, dad and younger brothers all about my experiences of the day. My mother did comment that this was the first time she had seen me after a fight without any marks to my face. We all had a good laugh and my brothers wanted me to tell them all about the day, all over again, Warts and all.

The following Tuesday evening's training consisted of an autopsy of my fight, and then I spent some time discussing and recollecting what I had learned from my first experience of competition. This took up most of the evening's session. This was the tradition; I was told, after any competition, whilst it was fresh in the mind. It made sense to me.

The four musketeers- Peter, David, Ray, and Alan

A few weeks later Benny called me to one side before training, and asked me to leave my kit at the gym. We were going to be taking a bus down to the Phoenix boxing club at Ickles, on Sheffield road." Why are we going there" I wanted to know. "I will tell thy on way down" he told me. We walked out of the square and turned right into Corporation Street to catch a number 69 bus to Ickles. Ickles is located just about two miles away, on the outskirts of Rotherham heading towards Sheffield. The bus, which was parked up directly across from the Odeon Cinema was displaying 'Sheffield' on the name plate at the front. The Odeon cinema, one of the oldest in Rotherham, boasted having the famous Wurlitzer organ, which would be elevated from down in the pits into full view, and reached the stage height. The organist would provide entertainment for the audience on a regular basis prior to the films being shown, I was wondering what was going on, and why we would be going to another boxing gym anyway. We sat down stairs on the bus that was now ready to leave. "Reyt" Benny said, as we both sat down and settled into our seats, "It's time for thee to move on, to where tha can make better progress than I can do for thy, Steelose boxing club" (which was the commonly known name for it in those days), "is abart best int country and tha will get looked after wi them better than I can do for thy." I felt sick, and dazed. If he had smacked me across my face it wouldn't have felt as bad. Tears were welling up, and I had to fight to keep the floodgates from opening. I looked away, out of the window so he couldn't see my face, I felt like I was being pushed away and abandoned. "Remember that question I asked thy a bit back," he asked me. And then without waiting for me to answer, "Well if tha wants what ah think tha wants, then this is what tha gunna after do to get it." I couldn't speak if I had tried too; I would have given away my feeling, and just nodded. I really did want to tell him that I would be more than happy to continue with him, and take my chances at the Red Lion Boxing Club. Why couldn't he continue to help me become a boxer? I didn't understand.

The bus came to a stop just a few yards past this big church-like detached building on the opposite side of the road, with large brown double doors at the top of a flight of three steps. Benny opened up one of the doors and half pushed me inside, my legs were not functioning properly at the time. My mind was working overtime, wondering what was going to be inside to greet me. The first thing I saw to my right was this lad Cloggy Clark who, a couple of months previously had given me a proper boxing lesson. He had then left the Red Lion club a few weeks later. Cloggy had turned to see who had come in through the door, and so had just about everyone else. I was introduced to a big strapping man, with shoulders like a barn door, who had come walking across the floor to greet us." Ray, this is Mr Pearson," said Benny. "Call me Jacky" he said, I suddenly recognised him from being in the opposite corner, at the exhibition bout with his lad a few weeks previously at the Red Lion." We have had a good talk about you" he said. "We would like you to join our club, and fight for us," I suppose it was a sort of question, which was not answerable, the way he had said it, other than me saying no, I don't want to fight for you, I am happy with what I have. I trusted Benny and realized that what was happening was probably necessary, in a strange way. I think I liked Jacky Pearson from the start, just the way he talked and he had made me feel important, as we spoke about me becoming part of the Phoenix Boxing Team.

9

Very familiar miles

Firbeck is a great sight. The street lighting creates this daylight effect, making the head torch redundant for a few minutes, but was soon back in use after leaving the church of St Martin's behind, and out across the open fields towards the hamlet of Stone. Firbeck has a large oval field in the village which was once the private racecourse of the 18th century legendary Anthony St Ledger, who originated the world famous Doncaster St Ledger horseracing event.

I always get the feeling of being on my way home from here, and soon that was about to happen, as I approached the very eerie shadowy ruins of Roache Abbey on my way to Maltby. Roche Abbey, built from local lime stone, was founded in 1147 on the north side of the river Beck which runs through the valley close to Maltby, with king's wood to the southwest. This Cistercian Monastery, built for the so called White Monks would have been located on the outskirts of the northern edge of Sherwood Forest and in a perfect spot due to an abundance of natural resources in the area; water, wood, and stone. It is reputed that Robin Hood went to mass here. The Abbey was destroyed as part of the Dissolution by King Henry the V111 which rendered the building into ruin. The Abbey is now a much frequented landmark for the tourist, and is in the hands of English Heritage.

Some twenty minutes later I passed through the church yard, and up through the lichen gate at St Barthomnue church. I passed my cottage and was now on solid tarmac for a change, I am very tempted to call in at home, but at this time in the morning just before 3am, I thought I'd better not. The reception would not be too good.

My cottage, built in 1872 of stone reputedly from the ruins of Roche Abbey, was originally the old village school. It was converted into a place of dwelling in 1982 and still retains most of the original features, with a particularly well preserved Canadian Maple floor, and large timber trusses to the underside of the exposed ceilings.

My next food stash was waiting for me just before reaching Braithwell Road, tucked under a large stone behind the farm buildings to my right. I prayed that this container would be intact and free from unwanted visitors. Lifting the lid off the box, I keenly investigated the small new potatoes with a mint sauce topping, it looked just fine. The minty smell fuelled my sense of hunger. I knew these small new potatoes would go down well and convert into fuel over the next hour or so. The box which I replaced back under the stone is probably still there. I will check the next time I am out training on this path, I am sure it will bring back great memories.

I had left Maltby well behind me now, and knew that in just a few more miles I would be back at the college, but I was also very conscious that there were still some difficult and challenging undulating miles to negotiate.

I felt relatively good and comfortable with the food and a drink of water containing a shot of concentrated electrolyte in it to keep the salt levels topped up. I experienced no problems from the blister on my foot at this point of the run; in fact my feet were in relatively great condition. I had just started to feel conscious of the mileage in my legs, but more than happy, as I made my way through the very quiet village of Micklebring, turning sharp left at the last house, down the very uneven field path, and then left along the hedgerow, and through the underpass of the M18 motorway.

As I ran parallel with the M18 motorway, I looked out for the rickety style that would take me right, across the fields towards the Willow plantation. I wondered if I would come across the herd of wild deer that I had seen during my recent training runs through the plantation and across these fields. Maybe they sleep at night.

It was very quiet as I passed by the Firsby Hall Farm, zigzagging along the wide track around the out buildings, and turning left and diagonally up the long path to the top of the field on the tree lined horizon. I needed a good degree of light as I made my way off the ridge line and down the path between the woods. It was always boggy, ankle deep, and very slippery down this path. I had been anticipating this decent well before getting here. Even in the summer it can be very treacherous because the deep muddy area covers the entire width of the path, leaving only the slippery tree roots to step on. I worked hard trying to keep on my feet, holding on to the trees at the sides and made slow progress on this very demanding downhill path. It was certainly impossible to keep my feet dry as I headed down towards the dry grassy path at the bottom, up the steep rise and then across the main Doncaster road at Hooton Roberts.

I started to feel like I had been awake for weeks; my eyes were tired and gritty, which was probably caused by the light from my head torch, as it cut through the darkness of the night, creating this never-ending tunnel, And the very bright glairing effect which bounced back at me whenever the beam hit a target to either side of the tree lined lane. This made me feel totally on my own as I reached this stretch of the route in the middle of nowhere. I made a stop, fuelled up, got my head into gear and got these negative feelings out of my system and focussed my mind on positive thoughts, I still had a long way to go.

The climbs were now over, and soon I was on my way down into Old Denaby, but felt the steep incline pulling at my lower back. I was glad when I reached the bottom of the grassy hill and came out of the corner of the field, this was to be the last check point in about fourteen hours, I hope.

I was now on firm tarmac; the street lights provided a well lit area for a change, and looked like civilization at last. There was just about three miles to the completion of the first fifty miles. I now felt very confident that I would be able to fulfil my ambition of completing 100 miles. I had that good feeling inside again; it seemed to have been working through ever since the last down beat spell half an hour ago. I headed down past Old Denaby, turned left towards the railway crossings and left again down the canal towpath.

The canal was lit up by the moon, and long shadows were being cast from the old warehouses across the water. I lost concentration and I passed the turn off to the left by the side of the concrete fish statue on the tow path. Just in time I realised my mistake, turned back and headed left up towards the train station. The path seemed unusually long this morning as I finally left the canal, and joined the river bank path, eventually reaching the end of the industrial area and leaving the path by the side of the large storage tanks, and at last onto the tarmac.

I headed out past the industrial estate and along the well lit road, passed Morphy Richards factory, on the left, looked for, and made sure I didn't miss the turn off, over the side of the railway bridge. I ran carefully down the steps and through the small housing estate, then back on to the old canal tow path through the car park of the derelict Ship Inn Pub at Swinton. The canal here has had a major face lift over the past couple of years making it very easy going on the wide tarmac path. I left the canal towpath behind and ran alongside the well lit football fields. I crossed the road and then got onto the narrow earth paths alongside the railway embankment. I could see the lights from the college on the horizon in front of me, as I came out through the wooded area and onto the cycle path. I headed down into the car park at Manvers College; it was slightly misty and eerie at that time in the morning with all the cars covered in dew. I finally passed what would be the finish line in the next twelve hours or so.

I experienced a feeling of elation. Would I really be able to complete the self inflicted challenge I had set, soon the second 50 miles would begin again, and I was under no illusion that the next time around would be less demanding.

It was very quiet as I reached the doors to the sports hall at Manvers College in Wath-upon-Dearn. It seemed so ironic to me that some fifteen to eighteen years ago, I spent almost two months of my working time supervising, and actually working here on this site, as my company erected the structural steel framework, which became the college and complex it is today, The main building, which is set out on different levels and forms a series of curved structures, with elevating towers separating the interlocking units, has now provided education for thousands of pupils over the years.

The security guy spotted me, and opened the doors gesturing me to keep quiet, I could see from the number of cars parked up that the hall would be full of sleeping competitors. He recognised me from yesterday. "You're the guy who's doing the double distance." I am famous at last, I thought. He opened the door and let me in.

I needed to wash, clean my teeth and completely change my kit; it was now about ten minutes to five am. The Rotherham Harrier race officials had started to arrive, and whilst I had a bowl of cornflakes and fruit, they set about organising the tables in readiness for the registration for the 50 mile main event. I collected my official race number "101" and T shirt. As I looked around the hall at the carpet of sleeping athletes, tucked up in their sleeping bags, bodies were beginning to stir, and I could see signs of life increase. Soon the odd noise grew into a buzz of voices and more activity from the athletes who were getting ready for the event that was about to take place in a relatively short time. Many of the athletes were aware that I was attempting a 100 mile feat and good luck wishes came in abundance. I was congratulated on completing the first fifty miles in eleven hours and forty minutes. I had completed the fifty miles a bit quicker than I had predicted, in well under twelve hours. At this stage I didn't feel any worse for the faster pace, but would I suffer later on the second 50 miles? I preferred not to dwell on this thought for long.

10
I meet my running mate in the desert

Race day 2 Wed 10th March

I woke up about 6am. My first sight of the occupants of our tent of sleeping athletes, mostly out in the open, but tucked up in their sleeping bags, brought the stark reality of what we endurance runners are prepared to go through to achieve our goals. I had been advised and had placed all my running kit, including shoes, inside my sleeping bag. It was safer than putting your feet into shoes and body into kit that might contain unwanted creepy crawlies which could have crawled in during the night. It was still freezing cold and the breath from us all was coming out like white mist.

There was no real rush to leave the sleeping bag, or to getting ready this morning and certainly no queue for the toilets, just a walk out into the desert in almost any direction. You could take your pick of which dune you fancied, this was the order of the day. White bums would appear and then disappear in a flash as the sun made contact with bare skin. During your own trip out, trying to pick a path to the dune of your choice without any embarrassing encounters became a big challenge. Breakfast would be served at about seven thirty as the site came to life with a buzz of exciting voices, either discussing yesterday's performances or what was about to confront us in today's leg of the race. I couldn't get my right shoe on because of the size of the bandage around my big toe, a bit of a panicky time, although I was more than prepared to run without the bandage. I revisited the doctor who strapped my toes together after breakfast and at this stage I had no pain at all, I couldn't feel my foot let alone the toe, so I was ready for the day's race without any real pain.

The 100 km Del Sahara race, is advertised as a trail running adventure, and is rightly called the flagship event of the Zitoway Sports and Adventure Company. The race calls for the physical and psychological ability to adapt and cope with the less than suitable conditions of running in the desert terrain. The heat or wind and weather conditions are harsh and unpredictable as I have found out to my cost. I needed to be resilient to maintain a mental toughness and bring out the hyper competitiveness in me, to get me through to the finish.

A good day for a run in the desert

The sun was already starting to lift the temperature and the slight breeze was beginning to feel hot, more like I had expected. As I walked across to join the runners for the start of today's leg, I could see the results of yesterday's run; people were hobbling, stretching and rubbing tired muscles.

On the start line the now familiar "We will rock you" was being played at the beginning of the shortest leg of the event; we were heading for Bir el Grijma about 18km away.

As I ran through midday my shadow became my one and only companion, although small in comparison to the vast area of the desert around me that was due to the sun sitting directly overhead, but still providing me with some small comfort, like having a pal along side. At this point of the run there was nobody in sight, either in front or behind. It now became a pure mental thing; you felt that you were the only person on the planet. Was I really heading in the right direction? I had lost sight of any directional flag on the horizon, and my hair stood up on the back of my neck with the realisation that I had suddenly lost touch with anything that provides a safety net. The mental anguish I was experiencing at this moment was striking a kind of fear in my mind as I looked around at this bleak barren landscape, questioning my navigational skills. "This is why I am here" came into my mind. At this point every breath I took felt like having my head in an oven, you tend to take shallow breaths to avoid the heat affecting the lungs, and the back of my mouth was dry. I was so glad I didn't have to talk to anybody. Well, apart from myself, and my shadow. There was no sign of life other than odd tracks of some small creature that had scurried away at the sight or sound of my approach. You can have prepared your training, and your kit, but if your mind is not functioning correctly, it will be an uphill task.

My shadow became my running mate, and travelling at a perfect pace. I was confident that all I needed to do was to keep following my shadow in front of me. We were attached, but also somehow separate. My shadow gave me focus through the vast and barren desert, of never ending yellow sand, which spreads out as far as you can see and disappeared into the horizon.

There was also a beauty in the desert that's so very different to any other place. I had never seen such a colourful and vibrant environment, which changed so quickly. Both in colour and texture.

At last I could see runners in front of me, and slowly started to catch up with a group of Italians, two women and three men. I was feeling good at this stage and pressed on, catching them up with about two kilometres to go. We ran together into our camp for the night. This time the site looked quite orderly. My tent, No25 which I shared with the five other mixed British runners was erected this time. We were directly opposite the first aid tent, which at this time of the afternoon had a fairly large gang of runners waiting to have blisters and sore muscles sorted. I joined the queue and was eventually sorted. That doctor had a magic touch.

My shadow & running mate

Whilst I was waiting my turn for treatment, I was talking to Patrick, Jose, and some of the other athletes about how to best deal with blisters, it was agreed by all that the best solution was to lance the blister with a needle, and make two holes, one top and one bottom. Squeeze and drain the fluid from the blister, fill the needle with neat iodine. Clench your teeth, take in a big breath, and then inject the neat iodine into the cavity between the outer and the raw skin... now "SCREAM," and swear like a Maltby Colliery coalface worker. It's best to have people around you , "so that they can tell everyone about your feats of heroism at a later date; leave to breath overnight, then tape over with Zink oxide tape, in readiness for the next day's running.

On my way back from the first aid tent I called in to the dinning tent and picked up a mug of coffee and a large slice of fruit cake for Kenwynne and me, one of our British ladies. Laying with our feet up and resting as best we could, 'as you do in the Sahara' talking about the running events that she had done, and wow, this lady had taken part in some amazing events. She is one of the only five woman in the world to have raced on every continent, including the Arctic and Antarctica. She has completed the Marathon-des- Sables' three times, this race, the 100km del Sahara five times, she had fairly recently ran from John o Grouts to Lands End, and was heading off in two months time to run three marathons in twenty four hours, in the Namibia desert. On and on she spoke of the races she had run in all over the world. Where does this ability come from? This seventy year old, frail looking woman with hardly what would be called an athletic frame, has just got to be one of the greatest distance athletes in the world. I was spellbound and could have listened to her for hours. I felt very inspired and privileged to be in the company of this incredible woman, and sharing a tent together. We have become good friends and contact one another frequently to discuss our running exploits.

The rest of the British athletes were all coping well with the conditions, and seemed to be free of the dreaded blister problems. Pat had perfected a taping system that she had successfully used on her feet over the years, and was in the process of expertly taping up Cliff's feet in readiness for the following day's leg of the race. Her theory was that friction evasion on the skin between the shoe and sock, would eliminate potential blisters. My own thoughts on the subject is, cocooning the feet in such a way that your skin cannot breath only makes for real sweaty conditions and attracts heat. My double skin socks provide the coolness of cotton with the movement between the skins of the socks taking out most of the friction. I just have to be aware and remove the sand from my shoes every now and then. I am no specialist on the subject and can only really comment on what works for me.

11
My apprenticeship

My parents had to be involved with my move to the new gym; they had to fill out the form and sign a consent form in agreement to the rules of the club, and I suppose some sort of indemnity, which they did without too much opposition. We had had an evening discussing the sport of boxing. My brothers Alan, who was a year and half younger than me, Peter, just over a year younger than Alan, and David the youngest, were all proud of their big brother and continually fired questions about what I felt like when I was in the ring. Was I scared, did it hurt when I was punched etc. We talked about my move from the Red Lion and discussed what it could mean for me joining my new club. I remember my dad saying that it could be a great opportunity for me and one which could automatically put me in line for a good job, if I was to stay at the club until I was ready for leaving school at fifteen. Steel Peach and Tozer was without doubt the biggest company in the area at that time, and employed over eleven thousand workers.

There was certainly a much more professional feel to my new coaching. The training at 'Steel'os', as it was affectionately called, felt much more regimented, like being in the army, I imagined, than the easier happy go lucky attitude at the Red Lion. I missed Benny Kemp so much during those first few weeks, and remember vividly his tearful parting words to me. "I will keep an eye on thy, iel always know what tha up to" he had said, and wished me luck, as he nearly squeezed the life out of me, and shook hands for the last time.

The advanced training disciplines were soon having a positive effect on my fitness level. Everything I was involved in, skipping, bag work, speed ball, and sparing, becoming much easier for me as I settled into the routine of learning my trade so to speak. Distance running was introduced into my fitness training at that time. I would run mostly off road, before and after school. Much before long I was completing up to fourteen mile a day. I hated running then, with as much passion as I love running today, but it did help to give me an abundance of stamina. I suppose it was a bit like serving as an apprentice.

"We need to get you kitted out because you're fighting in a couple of weeks "said Jacky Pearson one night," You will need vest, shorts, and boots and…" I stopped him from going any further." We won't be able to afford to get that lot," I remember saying. "You won't have too; I will give you a chitty to take down to Danny Williams' sports shop. They will let you have the gear, and the club will sort out the bill", he said. He then explained about the club being subsidised by the Steel Peach and Tozer social services. It seemed that every employee automatically had a few pence stopped out of their wages every week, which would then fund the operatic society, football, golf, weight lifting and boxing clubs. "We justify this funding by producing good fighters, who win more trophies than any other clubs around," he explained. I was informed that the club currently had seven ABA champions. "No pressure there then I thought."

That Saturday morning, armed with an envelope which contained this precious piece of paper, the 'Chitty'. I ran all the way down town and up Ship Hill to Danny Williams Sport shop, which was opposite Cooper's toy store. Danny Williams, who played right half, was a very popular and long serving Rotherham United football club player.

I walked into the shop, which wasn't busy at the time, and a middle aged woman asked if she could help, so I handed her this official requisition slip, which she looked at, and then asked what I would be wanting. I handed her a list of items that had been written down by Jacky during the evening, whilst I trained. She looked me up and down, disappeared, and then reappeared with an armful of vests, shorts, and socks. Try these on for size in the changing room through there, pointing to a curtain in the corner. What size shoes do you take, she asked, and disappeared again as I walked towards the changing room. The first pair of black shorts fitted me OK. The nearest fitting vest, which was the smallest they had, was a goldy colour and I reckoned could be altered to fit. Try these on for size, she said, handing me this box, containing a lovely pair of black leather boxing boots. "What size jock strap do you need?" She asked. I was speechless, and felt my face colouring up, as I totally misunderstood what she meant by size. We had talked about needing one of these supports to keep my dangly bits from swinging about whilst training, and of course fighting; I was now 'getting to that age', it was decided. How do I know how to measure what size I want. She could obviously see my embarrassment by the beetroot red my face must have turned to. She looked like she was having a fit trying to contain herself, and almost laughed out loud. As she turned back to face me, but this time she had a tape measure in her hand, managing to keep her face reasonably straight. I was mortified wondering what she was going to do with that measure, when she then asked what size 'Waist' I was? "Oh" the relief I felt. I bet she would have had many a laugh over the years, with that incident. I certainly have. The boots were too large, and the smallest they had in stock, but I was promised that they would order the size I needed, and would be available for me to pick up after school on Wednesday.

I had been playing football for my school, St Beedes RC, the following Tuesday afternoon at Kimberworth, and because the game didn't start until sometime after four thirty, I was later than my usual time of around six oclock getting down to the gym. As I opened and walked through the door I was summoned over by Jacky Pearson. He was in conversation, by the side of the ring, with one of the assistants, Jim, and the very smart light grey suited Jack Cox. I had met, and had been introduced to Jack Cox, the club manager, a few weeks ago. I had found out as time went on he was responsible for arranging and matching opponents for the club team. "You are fighting next Thursday at Pitsmoor working men's club" he said to me. "His name is Bruno. Coach leaves here at five thirty. Are there any problems?" This man never had much to say other than just what was needed. Jacky followed me into the changing rooms, and put me fully in the picture about the forthcoming event. Did I have my kit? he asked, and gave me a club badge, telling me to get it stitched onto my shorts, and not onto my vest. I had asked why? He explained the reason why. A badge is a target for your opponent to aim at he said. "Oh and there's room on the coach for your dad if he can make it."

The barber who worked in the shop at the entrance to the Red Lion Square was a boxing fan, and had been giving me and the lads from the Red Lion Boxing Club cheap haircuts every couple of weeks, had told me to keep coming even though I was no longer a member of the Red Lion Boxing club. I would have to sit and wait until any of his regular customers had been given cuts. I could never understand what he was talking about, when after finishing the men's haircut, he would ask them

"Anything for the weekend sir," disappear into the back, and then produce, and slide a small brown envelope into their hand.

One particular Saturday afternoon was to have a very memorable impact on me. He offered to give me a free haircut so that he could practice a new style that was coming in and supposedly sweeping the country. The American Crew cut. This style would be perfect for me, I thought. It would relieve me of the burden I went through every morning; of struggling to get the comb through my very unruly tight curly ginger locks, which would normally bring tears to my eyes. I felt very light headed as piles of my hair fell to the floor around me. He then proceeded to level off the three-quarter inch tufts left on my head. As I made my way home, everyone I passed it seemed, stared at the new me, it made me feel different, and sort of groovy. But my mother had different views on the cut, and threatened to go down to the shop and throttle the barber with her bare hands. My hair had been spoiled for the rest of my life, and would never look right again. But after a day or two she settled down, and came round to my way of thinking, that it suited me, and would be so much easier to manage. Gone were the evenings of reducing me to tears, at the weekly ritual me and my brothers went through, as one by one, we would kneel and place our heads onto a newspaper in my mother's lap. She would inspect and then drag the nit comb through my tangled hair, in the search for the little monsters that invaded my head from time to time. The sound of 'Gotcha' and a click as the insects were crushed by the force of her thumb nails grinding together was like the hunter getting the prize. We would be grilled on who we were sitting next at school. I had pioneered the new cut, which had become more acceptable and popular over the coming weeks, elevating me at school with my mates, as they all wanted to follow my lead. Week after week and one by one most of my mates ended up with the Crew cut, and eventually getting the length down to about half an inch.

My time at school seemed to be more pleasurable all round. I had learned to control my temper, and as part of the rules of the Phoenix Boxing Club, and the Amateur boxing Association, I had made a promise, never to take advantage of the new skills I was being taught, by using them outside of the ring. I had stopped being confrontational towards my classmates, and actually backed away from arguments. I think that the entire teaching staff, especially Mr Flynn, the much disciplined sports teacher, who was usually the first on the scene when any fight broke out, seemed to be so relieved at the 'New Me'. He would appear as if by magic, within a few seconds of a fight breaking out, with a set of boxing gloves in his hands, which he kept hung up on a wall in his office. They were needed quite frequently during my troublesome time at school; it probably seemed a waste of time putting them away whilst I was around. The offending pupils would be invited to either shake hands and walk away, or glove up and be invited to fight to the Queensbury rules, whilst a human ring was formed around the two fighters. The fight would last until one of them packed in; spurred on by the cheering ring of pupils. Gasping for breath was enough to end the fight, and normally after only a couple of minutes. One of them would have usually been me in the past, but it was never me that packed in first and called it a day. My mother also commented on how pleased she was, at not having to repair damaged cloths and tape up cuts and bruises. I think though, that life was probably more boring for the rest of my school mates as I knuckled down to my school work, instead of confronting anything that didn't suite me.

12
What's another 5 miles?

Shortly after five forty five am Saturday the 16th October, I set off again from Manvers College feeling incredibly confident that I would be successful in completing the first ever one hundred mile Round Rotherham. Can I contain this great feeling, convert it into energy, and slowly release it when I most needed it. I would wish that everyone could experience this brilliant feeling, and coming at a time when you are in sight of your special goals, sometime in their lives. This could be running a marathon for the first time, dropping a dress size, or caring for a sick friend or loved one. We all have our own boxes to tick, each one as inspirational and as important as the other. On the other hand, was it audacious of me to think that I would be able to take on this run and be successful, taking for granted my normally good health? We do have to believe in our body's capabilities of coping with whatever we demand, and lessen our fears of any new ventures, because we are generally only held back by fear of the unknown.

I let the officials know I was going to make a start, and as my time was already logged at five pm from the previous afternoon it wasn't necessary to formally set me off again. I set off in the dark and headed out on the road towards Wath, and passed the fire station again, reflecting on what I had felt like with Holly by my side, about twelve hours ago. I was now into a good steady pace; my legs were working pretty well without any signs of stiffness or fatigue. I was soon crossing over the bridge to get to the lake paths, which felt a bit slippery underfoot on the smooth surface. With head torch now switched on, I picked out the path alongside the manmade lakes at Wath-upon Dearne; I could make out the tents belonging to the night fishermen who commented on my being out running at an unearthly hour in the morning; some comments were unrepeatable but understandable because the dogs were making a real old racket. They were soon to be well and truly disturbed by hordes of athletes at full gallop. I wondered what comments they would make during the next hour or two. These guys were, I suppose endurance fishermen, as dedicated to fishing as we were to running. I remembered passing this group of men just over twelve hours before. I wondered if their night had passed as quickly as mine.

I reached the canal side and left Wath behind; my head torch gave a light that turned the path into a never ending tunnel. I was in automatic mode and had not really been concentrating for some time, oh what a massive mistake. I suddenly got the feeling that I was not where I should be. How long had I been running in this state of mind where you engage cruise control, relax, and just let the miles go by? Realising that I had completely missed the turn off from the canal, I guessed I must now be very close to Barnsley by the lights on the skyline in front of me. Not knowing whether the canal comes back onto the route, I felt such a fool as I decide to set off back, retracing my steps to join the correct path. It took me just over half an hour, and by the time I arrived at the turn off, there was a large group of athletes going through from the six o clock starters. This was the first time over the last twelve or so hours that I felt low. I estimated that the time lost would work out to at least five extra miles; this is not what I needed, but at the same time it made me more determined not to make such a stupid mistake again, after all I had run every one of these legs of the route dozens of times. I had to get this negative feeling out of my head, after-all what's another five miles?

Whilst taking part in any long distance race there is a constant internal voice, speaking to you especially at times like this. I needed to find, and switch on the power that makes the difference between my success or failure. There is always a price to pay. The bigger the challenge, the bigger the price you have to pay. At the time of thinking about running one hundred miles, I did realise that once I had mentally accepted the challenge, there would be times like this which may become even far more demanding as the miles went on. I knew then that I would be strong enough to get through any of these negative blips. Ultra distance running is a very individual sport; although you may have dozens of other athletes around, it's still a very lonely event and all down to you. I expected worse to come as this day unfolded, but I know that whatever comes I am confident that I will be ready to meet the challenge.

I was now on a mission to get myself back into that good feeling zone again. Catching and passing a steady stream of walkers before we reach the Elsecar woods provides me with the target, and a good steady pace sees me achieving the positive results I am after. The paths had dried out somewhat from the previous night, making it a bit easier going as I passed athletes steadily climbing up the rocky path away from the railway level crossings. I was now in front of a large group as we start to climb out of the woods, and head out towards Wentworth. The church spire was now in full view as I reached the open path. I could put away the head torch now; it won't be needed for some time.

Heading up the concrete drive towards the wood yard and just before the main road, the first of the main group of runners came past me at what seemed an incredible pace. These guys were flying and looking strong. Will this be the year for a new record for the 50 mile event? The record for the fifty mile distance in this event has stood since 1996, and was set by Chris Parkes, a member of Rotherham Harriers, in a staggering time of Six hours, seventeen minutes.

I passed the old Holly Trinity church at Wentworth; it dates from pre 14th century and was replaced with the newer one, which was more visible to the left now as we climbed up from the road. This has a large tower, and was built in around 1872 for William Wentworth, the 2nd Earl of Stafford.

There was now a steady stream of athletes coming alongside and passing me, as we approached and passed the pretty little stone built school on my left. This was where my granddaughter Holly was educated, before joining her current one at Wath. Must not get caught up in the faster speed at which these athletes are travelling, I must maintain this steady pace, otherwise I will run out of energy, and struggle to make the distance.

My phone started to ring as I headed up the hill towards Keppel Column, a much less imposing site in the daylight. It's Brian Harney, one of the Rotherham Harriers officials, wondering where I am, and checking that I am still in the event. When I give him the reason for my delay at reaching the first checkpoint, his comment is quite predictable, how the hell could I get lost, and miss the turn off?

As I turned out of the housing estate and headed down hill on the main road, I had dozens of athletes around me, as we dodged around the cars travelling up and down the busy main road. I saw the bewildered looks on the driver's faces. They must have wondered what the hell was going on, as hordes of athletes took over the road. We were soon turning into the golf course entrance, and then heading down the grassy bank to the first checkpoint at Grange Park.

There was a large crowd of athletes, spectators, and marshals gathered around the erected gazebo. I could hear the cheering and shouting of congratulations as I reached the gazebo and food table. An explanation of where I had gone wrong to Brian, brought comments of "Silly Sod", from one of the Kimberworth Striders runners, and other comments that are best left in my memory. My aim was to spend as little time at these checkpoints as possible, to try and maintain a reasonable average speed on this last fifty mile. I have a good amount of water in my camel back (A trade name for a water container of between one and two litres which is carried on the back like a rucksack). I had been nibbling food during the last five miles or so. All I needed was a small amount of food to top up, which I could eat as I ran., I picked up a large slice of fruit cake and a cup of orange juice and set off to a great cheer, heading out across the field at the back of the Rotherham Juniors football pitches, and down into the woods. I was feeling invincible right at this moment. As the saying goes 'This is as good as it gets."

Coming up the steep climb out of the woods, I headed out across the main road, looking up at the steep bank, and the climb in front of me, which some how this morning seemed to have grown steeper. For the first time my legs are started to feel the fatigue and pain of the miles that I had covered so far, and now with hands on my burning thighs I steadily made my way up this very demanding footpath. Climbing to the hilltop at Kimberworth, the runners were now coming past in a steady stream. These guys made it look so easy.

The very steep path down to meadow bank road started to cause me some pain in my lower back, which I hadn't felt for some weeks. I have a lower disc problem that I can usually manage to keep under control with daily pain killers. It had to be a posture problem, and made me more conscious of correcting the way I was running; standing more upright and taller. I gingerly made my way down towards the almost concealed entrance on Medowbank Road, which would take me down to the canal and towpath below. I managed to attract the attention of a couple of runners who had gone down towards the Rother Boiler Company, and sailed past the almost invisible entrance to the winding path, which they should have taken. As they caught up and came past me later on, heading out towards the Viaduct at Tinsley, I received a pat on the back together with their thanks. I know what it feels like to have gone adrift and miss turn offs that add miles to your run. Just about the same time two lady friends, from my running club (Maltby Running club) come along side me. Caroline, who had actually won the ladies event in the past; three times I believe, and who was now running her tenth outing of this full fifty mile race, would become the first female to achieve this number of runs. Alongside Caroline was Barbara, who was attempting her first running of this event, what a contrast. They both look pretty comfortable and like all female athletes they were holding a good conversation. "How do they do that?" We shared a couple of minutes running together. I wished them both well, before they made their way along the towpath, and slowly disappeared into the distance.

I was still being encouraged by friends as they passed by me and left me. My problem with this situation was not to get complacent and be pulled along at a pace that didn't suit my plans. It was great to hear another friendly voice, as Phil Haigh, another of the Maltby club members, and a very good friend, caught up with me as we reached the main road not long after coming off the towpath at Tinsley. Phil, who was running with John Kirk and Richard Hawcroft, spent a short time with me as they ran alongside for a few hundred yards. Christine Kirk, John's wife, and Adele, Richard's wife, were not far behind I was told, as I enquired about their whereabouts. The ladies soon caught up, and ran with me for a spell, talking about how I had coped with the night's session before slowly increasing pace and running away from me. We had trained together and covered a good number of miles over the past weeks leading up to this event. But today was all about my challenge, and almost to the point of being unsociable, but I still needed to be competitive. If I was going to complete the distance I needed to be totally single minded. I knew they understood, as they slowly disappeared past the Pike and Herron pub towards the turn off on Bawtry road.

Treeton checkpoint was my next fuelling station, and as I approached the cricket ground again I could hear the cheers for me as I came over the bridge into view. A few of my friends, who were taking part in the ladies' relay team event, gave me a great welcome just before I reached the check table. I felt like an Olympic champion.

These friends are all female members of my local gym, most of these women, who almost a year ago where none runners had never even managed one mile. The team; Fay, Louise, Samantha, Maloney, Joanne, Elly, Justine and Sam E, were now running out of their skins and in third position, just behind Rotherham Harriers, and Kimberworth Striders ladies. I am so proud of them all and the competitive spirit of this team of ladies is brilliant. They were providing support and comradeship for one another, together with some great support themselves from Helen and Anne, who had trained with us all over the months and are ready to step in should one of the team be unable to make it. It looks like they had been running together for years. Watch this space for next year.

The second checkpoint was manned by David Haywood, one of the Rotherham Harrier officials who were there to see me off the previous evening. I knew he was pleased that I was still on the move and likely to complete the distance. He shouted good wishes as I left to refill my larder at the food table, which was set up about ten feet away and just inside the Treeton Cricket Clubs car park.

Topping up my camel back water bladder to the brim, eating a couple of small boiled new potatoes, a generous slice of fruit cake, a bread and jam sandwich, together with a cup of hot coffee. I set off feeling stiff and tight around my lower back, after being stood for a while. Up past the cricket ground, and right down towards the lakes at Rother Valley Country Park, for the second time, I felt grateful that I had the ability to eat and run without encountering digestive problems. This leg was the next to the longest of the race; I headed off to Harthill, approaching the viaducts on the wide path. There was now a group of steady running athletes in front of me, providing me with my next target. My pace was down to a very steady jog/walk, it seemed easier for me to mentally relax for a while and just move at a slower pace but making progress nevertheless. I was hopefully recharging the batteries. By the time we reached the lakes at the Rother Valley Country Park, I was level with the group of five athletes, and stay with them for the next couple of miles.

Two of the guys were having blister problems and started to struggle. It was time to make a move; I was getting caught up into a slower, just walking pace, and set off with a steady jog. I felt better for the extra effort, which brought relief and provided a sort of rest situation to muscles that have been working overtime for a long time. By the time I reached the motorway bridge just before Woodhall Village, looking back there were no athletes in sight. I felt better for that little bit of self inflicted competition.

I was right about the nettles the previous night; they were now flat to the ground and no longer posed a threat as I turned between the houses and crossed over the style. The horses in the field were no longer interested and didn't even turn a head to see who was upsetting their normally quiet existence. The village of Harthill came into view at the top of the hill in the distance, this was my next checkpoint. Over the last couple of miles I had been on the lookout for signs of the owl that gave me a buzzing during the night. I could see areas of old stone buildings that could be home to the kamikaze bird; it would always be a point of interest for me from now on when I was in this area on training runs.

13
Dune, but not out

Race day 3. Thursday 11 March.

Today we were heading out to Bir el Kacem, with a distance of 42km, making it Marathon day, but if we are going to be right, due to the terrain, a more accurate distance of 44km is what I had been told we would be running, by the race, and course setter Carlos Garcia Prieto. Well fed, watered, and toe sorted, I stood on the start line, the now very familiar and stirring music "We will rock you "banging out through the large speakers brought a lump to my throat. Looking round at the gang of runners, all had made it to the start line, after the doctor had sorted out their individual problems. I wondering what they would be thinking today, tackling the longest leg of the race. I was feeling good with no worry about making the distance; in fact I was feeling quite strong and again no pain at all. I would like to think I was in control, but it was more than likely the pain killing injections

The gun sounded 'Here we go'. Off we went, but not as fast as usual, the much younger, stronger athletes, really were slower today. Maybe the heat, the distance to go, or as I thought to myself it must be me getting faster.

Today the large sand dunes were in front of us, and what a sight they were in the distance. As I got closer I remember looking up at the first 35ft dune wall, which had athletes in various positions of climbing the dune. From what I could see, there were a few fatigued runners nearing the top of the dune, and heading for the bright Zitoway flag that was blowing in the breeze. This was going to be an unavoidably tough climb, the only way we would be able to see which direction to take, would be to summit the dune.

I set about the first dune and quickly realized that I was not making much progress at all. I felt a bit like a hamster in a wheel, it was soul destroying, hardly gaining any height with each step. I remember thinking this was one of the hardest running climbs I had ever done, but then, that's why I was there in the Sahara Desert knowing that it would not be easy. If it was, then I probably wouldn't be there anyway. I believe my body was more than capable of coping with this challenge and the need to touch my true limits had not yet been reached in this race. Was I about to find out?

For me, there's always this subconscious ongoing dialog taking place on these endurance runs, which continually feeds my mind with the positive thoughts, and provides me with the strength and attitude I need to overcome whatever obstacles I meet. I don't have idols or mentors anymore. But I do draw on the experiences of my early boxing and the teachings I benefited from with my coaches, who have unfortunately all passed away, and of course my own imagination, which provides me with a constant source of inspiration.

I looked around from the summit of that first dune at the waves of beautifully sculptured and unspoilt sand dunes, which were now scarred by the trampling of deep footprints from the hoards of athletes as they attempted to reach the summits of these forbidding obstacles. Once on top, the secret to running the big dunes was to navigate around the peaks, and not dropping down into the troughs, as I soon learned, tumbling head over heels down from the top of the first one and lying at the bottom, looking up to the surrounding peaks of the dunes. Not feeling daft because there was no one about to see what must have looked quite funny. I certainly had a laugh laying spread eagle, looking up to the next dune to be climbed and the only way out.

The trouble with the practical side of keeping to the tops of the dunes was that I probably ended up running an extra 5km or so.

The dunes stretched on for miles, and soon I had spotted runners dotted about in the distance, I was catching up. My navigation of the dunes was working, or was I getting faster? Passing runners that I had not seen before in the race was very uplifting, and gave me a real adrenaline boost. This distance gave me time to experiment with ways of dealing with the heat; breathing through my head scarf, adjusting my pace and playing mind games with regards to the distance and fatigue, pretty much like the long training runs at home. The dunes finally gave way to a flatter terrain at last. After some seven hours the next camp site came into view.

I had survived and was still feeling quite strong, with only my toe giving me some pain now from the big sand dunes. I began to pass more runners, and finished the day at some speed through the finish line. I was feeling on top of the world. Although the softness of the sand does take you into a more fatigued state, you don't suffer from the pounding that your whole body takes, from running on tarmac during city marathons. The camp looked a very calm and inviting place as I made my way through the finish line of this leg.

There were groups of athletes laid about in front of the tents, all around the site. Massaging or being massaged, drinking, eating, and generally chilling out in this tranquil setting after the day's event and was at times like this you realised that all these comes about because of the brilliant organisation, which is further enhanced by the more than willing group of staff, who make the big difference to the smooth, efficient and successful running of this camp. These dozen or so helpers, who seemed to have a permanent smile on their faces, worked tirelessly to make sure that all the athletes received this five star treatment. Well, that is if you don't count the accommodations, but the Nomadic style shelter added that certain sort of magic to the event.

Did I mention the shower block? Well, each day we were able to take a shower from a water tank that had been erected just on the edge of the camp. Perched on top of a few scaffold tubes, was this large tank of water with about six plastic pipes connected to it, with a tap on each pipe. The water was always cold. How was that possible? But very welcoming, and as if to reiterate that we were all classed as athletes, not men and woman, there was no screening. So each afternoon without any formality and so natural as if this was a normal thing we athletes do every day, we stripped off and showered in this communal facility without a blush between us. Well, maybe a little one, ah ah.

That afternoon whilst having my toe sorted out, the first aid tent looked like a battle field inside. Laying on one bed to my right was a very distraught looking man with a space blanket wrapped around him, and a drip being fed into his arm. Inside the tent on the desert floor lying curled up and shivering, was a young woman, with a space blanket wrapped around her. One of the medical staff was helping to get her drinking water. An Italian runner was helped into the tent, and laid out on the table at the side of me, his left shoe was removed followed by his sock, and almost the entire sole of his foot came away in one big blister. The doctor cut the end off, which was hanging and attached to his heal, sprayed his foot with neat iodine, I am sure he was levitating above the bed for what seemed like minutes. 'He did finish the race,' I remember thinking, what am I concerned about, my toe is so insignificant at the side of some of the horrific blisters and muscle damage to quite a number of the runners. It did seem that today's distance had produced a lot of damage. I actually felt a bit of a cheat at this stage, taking up space and time that could be used to treat the badly damaged athletes who were waiting to be patched up.

All good friends together. Jose Luis, Cliff, Ray, and Patrick

The men and woman whom I met at this event were not like most other sports people I generally came across. They were not supermen or superwoman, they didn't profess to be either, but they do perform super feats of endurance and were able to blank out pain to achieve the end goal. Nationalities blended together in a common bond as we became a community of athletes, all out to help and assist one another, unselfish with advice and friendship, sharing food and shelter. What better reason could I have, to be part of this inspirational group of men and woman? That's why I was out here, to be among people like these athletes who push the limits to extremes and even then get that bit more.

After the magnificent suppers we had, the evenings were spent around the camp fire, with people playing guitars, singing and so intent on having a good time, forgetting the aches and pains of the event. We watched the spectacular sunsets, as this big red ball slowly sank into the horizon, casting bright red shadows along the desert sand, followed quickly by darkness. Then, as if someone had just thrown a big switch, the night sky lit up and produced this amazing display of shooting stars in the unpolluted sky. This was just an incredible sight, with billions of stars, lighting up the desert sky. Most of the major constellations were so visible and seemed so close, almost to the point of being able to touch them. The game of naming each one passed many hours. It seemed like this was our own very special display. I felt extremely privileged to be there witnessing our very own extraordinary aerial display every night. This spectacle was priceless and will be with me till I die.

14
I become a member of the boxing team

The big day finally arrived and for me that Thursday at school had been a bit of a haze. I couldn't concentrate on any of my lessons during the day, not even football, which would normally have had more than my full attention. Walking down into the town centre from our house in Masbrough with my Dad carrying my kit bag to catch the number 69 bus to the gym, we talked about how I was feeling going to my first fight. I think he was more nervous than I was. The bus ride to Ickles was soon over and as we approached the gym I could see this massive new shiny coach waiting outside. I introduced my dad around to everyone as we boarded the coach and sat down. There was more than enough room to spread out in the very luxurious interior of this impressive coach. I had only ever been on an old Charabang of a bus before during the last Brown Street working man's club outing to Skegness.

We travelled in luxury to Pitsmoore working men's club in Sheffield, almost in silence. I think my dad was struggling to say the right words to me and for my part I just wanted to be quiet and left alone in my own zone. I could always talk comfortably, openly and at any time with Mum, but found it difficult to open up to my dad. To be honest, in those days, kids were expected to be seen and not heard. "Don't bother your dad," was a much used phrase in our house, especially after he had started a new job and came home after a hard day's work.

We all congregated outside the Pitsmoor working men's club, after getting off the coach. We formed a group, and walked inside through the doors in a sort of military style line. It was very much like I had seen at the Red Lion that Saturday afternoon, a few months earlier and the effect had created about the same response. All eyes were turned towards us, but there were many more fighters tonight, and judging from the reactions of the crowd inside, we must have looked a formidable sight walking through that door, and this time I was part of that spectacle.

Inside the hall, as we walked to our dressing room, I could see the elevated ring was set up, and dominated the middle of the room. A large section of the seating was already occupied making the room look enormous. I was now feeling so nervous that it was difficult to walk, and breathe normally. I seemed to be staggering and bumping into the chairs that were set out towards the back of the room. I got the feeling that we had arrived a bit late, as we were ushered to our changing room in a bit of a rush by the Pitsmoor organisers.

"Ray, get ready, you're on first. Give me a shout when you're ready, and we will get you sorted with the doctor," said Jacky. I was in that daze again, and changed into my kit without actually realizing what I was doing. I was wondering what had happened to my dad, and was told that he was seated in the VIP seats. It took me ages to find out what that meant.

Once again I was caught up in that tornado, where everything is moving at a hundred miles an hour, and out of control. My kit, all new, seemed strange to me, and whilst I must have looked the part, I certainly didn't feel the part. The only thing that felt dead right was my new shorts. My vest had been tied at the back by Jacky, to stop the straps coming down over my shoulder, and my new boots felt large and clumsy. It was a lesson to be learned for the future–new kit must be bedded in before using for a competition.

I could hear the compare on the mike, ONE, TWO, ONE, TWO, and then with thumbs up from Jacky, as we stood by the dressing room door. The compare started the evening off with a bit of small talk whilst we waited to make a move. He then proceeded to announce my name first, and then my opponents, as we took that long walk down the avenue of seated spectators to the ring. Jacky, with his hands on my shoulders and about a foot behind, was talking to me all the way down to the ring side. It felt like he was steering me like a car and stopping me from wobbling into the seated spectators. Could he feel me shaking I wondered?

As I entered the ring, I could feel the heat from the bright arc lights on my head, which were suspended above the centre of this enormous ring. Looking across my opponent had not yet arrived in the ring, but I knew that he was on his way as he was being cheered coming through the home crowd supporters." Come on Bruno" was being chanted, and if they think I was being intimidated, well yes I was. But this time apart from the dry mouth I had, and butterflies in my stomach, I was feeling less like doing a runner than before. I was also giving myself a good talking to and mentally convincing myself that this boy in the opposite blue corner (I was in my favourite Red corner), was not going to give me any problems.

We were called to the centre of the ring by the immaculately dressed referee. Starched white shirt, black trousers with a crease that would cut you open if contact was made and the shiniest pair of black shoes I have ever seen. The instructions almost to the letter of the first ones I had heard were given and this time my opponent, Bruno was not avoiding my eye contact. "Back to your corners, and come out fighting," were the referee's final instructions. As I turned and headed back to my corner and Jacky, I couldn't help but think about the size of Bruno's nose. It's going to be a great target, I was thinking.

'Fast hands and move' was my first ever fight instructions from Jacky Pearson, as he gave me water to drink. "Seconds out, Round One." The bell sounded for the first round, and I heard my dad for the first time. "Come on Ray" he would normally call me by my Sunday name, Raymond, as the referee moved away from the centre of the ring. Bruno didn't make much movement towards me, making it easy for me to dominate the crown of the ring immediately, which made me feel in control right from the start. I don't remember going from nervous and wobbly legged, to feeling dominant and totally in control of the fight, but that's what happened, it was like a switch being flicked on. It's a dream start for me as I find gaps through his defence with ease. Before the end of the first round, the referee had stopped the fight due to a bad nose bleed. There was blood all over the ring, his vest, and even on my arms and vest. He was sent back to his corner to be looked at, whilst I retired to a neutral corner, waiting for his corner men to stop his bleeding nose. I couldn't help but feel sorry for him, as I looked across and out of the ring. I now felt a bit like being in a goldfish bowl, trying to locate where my dad was sitting. It was not possible due to the darkness of the hall and the brilliant lights shining down from above the ring. I was called back to the centre of the ring again by the referee to resume the fight, as Bruno came out of his corner. I really didn't have the heart to aim at his nose again for the rest of the first round. He looked terrified as we resumed the fight, and just backed away for the remainder of the first round.

Jacky didn't come into the ring at the end of the first round, but delivered his instructions to me from over the top rope, as he stood on the two foot wide apron outside the ring. The stool which would normally be waiting for me in my corner at the end of the rounds was not used, as I stood facing him. My fears and concerns had all turned to confidence, as Jacky calmly led me through my instructions for the next round, during the first minutes rest.

The second round started with a lot more movement from Bruno, but without any real attack. I was secretly inside having a good time, and feeling on top of the world, following my instructions, and using the fight to try some of the moves I had been taught during my training. The referee stopped the fight again, midway into the round, inspected Bruno's nose, and walked him back to his corner where his trainer wiped away the blood again. The referee inspected his face; brought us both together in the middle of the ring, and asked me to avoid contacting Bruno around his face or he would have to stop the fight, to save him any further damage. I nodded, seeing the fear in Bruno's eyes. I felt sorry for him; he must be feeling horrible; I never want to be in his position.

At the end of the round, I walked across to my corner feeling jubilant. Jacky enquired what the referee had said to me during the stoppage. He was spitting blood, at the comments from the referee, and explained that I was not to back off, this is a competitive fight, and I was there to compete for a win. Would my opponent offer me the same get out, if the boot was on the other foot? "No! so step up the work rate and let's get out of here." I felt sorry for Bruno, and what I was about to do in the next and last round. But my orders are part of what makes the difference, sometimes, between winning and losing.

Within a minute into the third round, the referee stepped in-between us, and the fight was stopped, announcing to the crowd that it was over as he escorted Bruno back to his corner. Blood was freely pouring out from his nose, which was also splattered all over me. I could see his trainers working overtime to stem the blood, right up to the time we were called to the centre of the ring for the announcement. The new ritual of standing in the middle of the ring, with the referee in between the both of us at the end of a fight holding on to my left hand and Bruno's right, as the announced was made by the compare that I had won on a technical knockout, the fight being stopped to avoid further punishment to my opponent. My arm was raised, and the crowd clapped, with one or two actually cheering. I really did feel sorry for Bruno, as I walked around the referee, and then putting my arms around his shoulders we walked over to his corner to shake hands with his coaches. His face and in particular his nose which was still bleeding slightly, looked bright red and sore.

I spotted my dad, as I left the ring, and was steered towards a large table full of prizes. It was my first choice between a writing case, and a box of glasses. I picked the bright red writing case, which I still use today. We were then directed out through the crowd towards the dressing room. The look on my dad's face told me all I wanted to know, as he mouthed to me "Well done."

My team mates were all over me as I walked through the door to change. I loved this game, and wanted more, was all I could think of. I was elated. Great start for the teams challenge, I was being told by Jim, our second in command, whilst being interviewed by the Phoenix Gazette reporter for the first time ever. Simon would be there at many of my fights to come.

We "the team" were having a great night, winning all but one out of the first five bouts up to the interval. The hall seemed to change in size as the lights went on for half time. I had located where my dad was sitting, and managed to get a seat next to him. I felt like a celebrity as the crowd moved to let me through, patting me on the back and saying well done as I passed by each one. I had expected a bit of hostility from the local crowd, but they showed totally different feelings towards me. This venue and crowd would become a home from home to me over the next few years.

I sat in the crowd with my dad for the entire second half, and witnessed my team mates performing against some great opponents and coming out with flying colours, losing only two of the thirteen bouts. It was a real eye opener as the more experienced fighters went about their business, dealing with a variety of different styles and skills. Jacky Pearson worked tirelessly in the corner to instruct and guide the lads through, round by round. We have a great team and many ABA champions. I sat there, cheering, feeling proud to be involved and watching my club mates perform.

I met up with Bruno to say my goodbyes before we left. He introduced me to his older brother and was pleasantly surprised at his attitude towards me. He congratulated me on my performance against his brother, shook my hand and wished me luck for the future. How good is Amateur Boxing, when you can show this genuine friendship, after competing against one another. Bruno's brother was one of the fighters who had won against our Middleweight. I was never to fight Bruno again, but we did become friends, as we met up at these local fight events over the coming years.

15
It's time to dig in deep

I was walking now more than running feeling leggy tired. My first feeling of distress came as I slipped whilst coming over the style at the bottom of the field just below Harthill. My foot shot away on the muddy plank, I came down on the hard ground with a jolt and my right leg muscles have locked up solid. The pain from my calf, which now looks so deformed, it almost looks like I had an implanted tennis ball under the skin where my calf should be. The pain was excruciating and the muscle in my shin now looked like a solid steel rod, which was pulling my foot into a deformed cramp, it was really horrible. I had this sickening feeling in my stomach, and no amount of massaging made any difference. Cursing for all I was worth, but knowing that I had to relax and wait for the muscles to settle, which seemed like hours, but infact, probably only took just a few minutes. Oh the relief as the muscles eased back to their normal shapes, it was better than winning the pools, as they say. Sweat poured out of me freely, wetting my shirt through. My mind was all over the place at this time, had I reached my limit? Is this where parts of my body would rebel and refuse to keep going? This was certainly a new experience for me. I was this so called 'tough guy' that never experienced problems of this sort. I was now hoping and praying that this was just going to be a one off. I had to dig in deep and get my mind into a positive state as I set off up the hill to the Harthill checkpoint. I certainly couldn't stop here all day. As I walked and nursed my right leg as though it was broken, but I felt better and more confident with each stride up the hill. There was one more style to negotiate half way up the hill and a big sigh of relief as I safely stepped down onto the grass at the other side. At last reaching the playground area and then up the ramp to the community hall checkpoint, it felt like reaching the safety of a harbour during a bad storm.

Checking in, but only drinking water, and eating a bread and jam sandwich, I was soon ready to go again. There were a couple of athletes who had pulled out of the race through injuries, one of them a young woman had a badly swollen ankle. They were sat in the hall waiting to be taken back to the college. I stayed only a few minutes at Harthill, knowing that I needed to keep on the move and reduce the risk of my legs ceasing up. Crossing the road and climbing up the steps, then the steep concrete path to the fields above, had activated the pain in my right calf again. I had to stop to give the muscle some vigorous treatment for a minute or two, this seemed to work. Again, stride after stride I began to feel better, but why was I getting cramp? I didn't ever suffer like this. I must be dehydrating, which has reduced my body salt. A shot of electrolyte in my water could be the answer. It was a good possibility and could be the solution to my worrying problem. Pouring a couple of shots into my camelback made me feel more confident that I could overcome this problem. It was time to take a good mouthful and must remember to do it regular over the next couple of hours.

It was now raining heavy, crossing the fields towards Netherthorpe, I had had a warning the rain was coming and had put on my wet coat. Zipped up and hood at the ready, the sky was now full of dark menacing looking clouds which were heading my way. Shortly I could see the rain coming across the horizon towards me. Before long the heavy rain started hammering down, this turned into hail stones within about ten minutes. The wind had also increased with the hail and was making a loud drumming noise on my coat. It was now bleak and more difficult to see where I was heading across the open field. Shelter was just less than half a mile away at Turner wood, but by the time I reached the hamlet the weather had just about subsided.

I was feeling cold, uncomfortable and to be honest, downright miserable at this time. I felt absolutely drained for the first time since starting out. This was probably about the time when it was both mentally and physically easier to give in, than to keep going. I realised that I had not been eating or drinking for the last four or five miles. I needed to sort myself out and get this negative situation out of my head. Food would help to rectify that problem I was experiencing. With some Christmas cake and an energy drink inside me I was feeling better already, I thanked John again out loud for the supply of the fruit cake from last night; although it would still take a few more minutes for the food to kick in and convert into energy.

Evaluating my situation, I had decided that with Woodsetts being about twenty minutes away, I would have to make warming up a priority, or I will more than likely end up with muscle damage, and then real severe problems. I was already stiffening up with the cold and starting to feel shivery. I knew that I would have to make the extra effort, and start running at a steady pace. I was confident that if I could get my heartbeat raised and body warmed up my body would become more efficient.

My right hamstring and lower back felt as though they were about to seize up as I made the initial surge, and started running again, but I realised that stiffness was what was causing my concern. I had to relax and run more upright. It started to work and after a while, although I was feeling tired and breathing heavy, I really did feel much more comfortable and relaxed in my body. The right calf felt just fine and less of a problem than previously. Maybe the electrolyte has kicked in and had started to circulate around my body. It was time to take another good mouthful and get my hydration level back up.

A new route under the A57 had been provided by the Carlton in Lindrick golf Club, and so instead of the Kamikaze-like dash across the very busy A57 main road, there was now access for the golfers and pedestrians, through a foot tunnel to the other side of the road. I had in the past had to stand and wait for a gap in the traffic for quite a considerable time before being able to cross over the busy main road, which splits the golf course in two. I took the newly painted underpass and crossed over the golf course, on to the other side of the road, then up and over the hill and down to the scouts hut at Woodsetts.

Woodsetts was always a very welcoming check point, the officials and ladies put themselves out to provide the best of food and drink, nothing was too much trouble for them and this really was very much appreciated I am sure by all the athletes. To have hot soup available together with the usual energy giving food and drinks was such a blessing.

I had my bag of spare clothes waiting for me, which had been brought through from the start at Manvers College, but apart from changing my top which was soaking with sweat from the effort of a few minutes earlier, the rest of the gear was put back into the plastic bag and placed on the pile for return to the Manvers College. I had made the decision that as my feet were feeling exceptionally good; I would leave what I had on. I felt it better not to risk upsetting what was working for me, and there was now only about twenty miles or so to go. Wow how good is that!

16
The brutal dunes need to be conquered again

Race day 4 Friday 12th March: Today we had about 25km to go heading out to Douz. Within a few kilometres we were into the big dunes again, this time even softer sand, bleached almost white, with a beauty unlike anything I have ever come across. The dunes had this rippling effect on one side of the peak which is probably caused by the influence of the winds, almost like the beach after the tide had gone out, but certainly harder than before to negotiate and climb. I was now after about ten km of running, among five or six runners all deciding that the routes they had picked to navigate these monsters was the best. It must have looked a strange sight with every one running in different directions. A bit like ants running around on an anthill, yet we all ended up in the same place eventually.

The cheering and laughter when one runner tumbled into the bottom of a dune was another memorable moment. The camaraderie was something very special. Remembering what it felt like, I knew what he was going through. He was laughing right now, but the poor guy would have to climb out of that unforgiving dune, which I knew would wipe the smile from anyone's face before reaching the top.

The heat of the sun was now hotter than I had experienced before. The need to keep covered but loosely, so as not to get burned is a must for my skin, letting the breeze pass around my head and body. The daily ritual of smothering all the exposed parts of my body in a very high factor suntan lotion was definitely one of the smartest things I had carried out. The pact I had made with myself to drink at least every 10 minutes, whether I felt thirsty or not, was also paying off. You don't feel or realise that you are sweating; it dries almost instantly on you, providing little evidence of what is actually taking place. It's only when you see all the salt on your skin at shower time that you realise how dehydrating the sun can be. I could actually scrape the white film of salt off my body at the end of the day's run. I was beginning to manage the heat better at last. The last leg of the race was going well, although hot, I was feeling pretty good and more acclimatised.

In the distance I had spotted a lone athlete on the horizon and due to the fact that I was catching up pretty quickly, I suspected that there must be a problem. Then with about eight miles or so to the finish I caught up with the runner, who turned out to be a young German woman. She had her shoes strung around her neck; her feet were covered in blood, and her socks torn to shreds. Assuring me she would make it to the finish, and gestured for me to go on. I just knew and understood, she needed to be on her own to deal with things in her own way. I could see in her eyes that she didn't want any sympathy from me, and would come through this problem in her own way. I had known before reaching her that there was something wrong, I was catching up far too quickly, and could tell from her body language she had a serious problem

I remember thinking as I left her, what would it feel like to be held down, and have the bottom of your feet scrubbed for an hour or two with sand paper, well that is what she was going through I thought. What a strong minded woman, she will be blanking out the pain, and certainly doesn't need any sympathy from me.

I was now on firmer sand, making good progress, catching and passing runners, who were now showing classic signs of fatigue as the finish line came into sight on the horizon. I could see the coloured blow up structure, like a large bouncy castle blowing about in the breeze. What a great feeling I was experiencing, yet it was a strange feeling at the same time, I wasn't hurting, and not really tired, I wasn't sore or blistered anywhere, and strangely I didn't want this race to come to an end.

It was now time to get out the Union Jack flag I had carried with me from the start of the race, just for this special occasion, where I could now run in looking like a proper British athlete. This was the vision I had imagined and dreamt about, when I first thought about entering this race.

The cheers that met me as I came in towards the finish was absolutely brilliant, all the finishers were lined up cheering everybody as they crossed the line. My feet felt as though they were not actually touching the ground as I crossed over the finish line. I was as high as you could get 'legally'.

The medal was placed around my neck, together with very warm hugs, and slaps on the back that would normally have felt like punches. Congratulations from all the staff as they held out fruit cake, oranges and tubs of water. A quick drink, dump the heavy rucksack, a hose down and then line up with everyone to greet the rest of the incoming runners.

Shortly after, the German woman came into view, she still had her running shoes round her neck, her feet were bleeding and the right heel almost down to the bone from the abrasive sand, Wow my toe hardly seems worth mentioning at the sight of this woman's feet, and a lot of the other runners damaged feet as they crossed the line.

I had managed to come through this race without sustaining one single blister; the sand gaiters that had been donated to me by NewBalence had certainly done the job. Nothing keeps out the sand entirely, so anything that helps is a great bonus.

The race was over and at its end, but no matter what language they spoke, everyone communicated with one other, in a bond like no other, and friendship that will last a lifetime. This race had brought together some very special people, we all shared this adventure in a spirit that only people who have lived, raced together, and shared the emotions of battling the desert and what it brought out in all of us. I think we all learned something about ourselves over this week in the desert. I did leave with a greater understanding about myself.

The end of the race was celebrated at the Hotel Sahara- Douz, later that night the whole event finished with a magnificent banquet. God only knows what we ate; if the shape of some of the meat was anything to go by. Well, I will leave you to guess. The prize giving was also charged with emotion, and the closing ceremony which was indeed a brilliant spectacle of an ancient tribal ceremony; involving almost white racing camels, Arabian horses, dancers and drummers, it was indeed something special.

'A city marathon will never quite look the same again after this magnificent adventure.'

We all said our goodbyes, exchanged Email addresses, telephone numbers and vows to keep in touch, both laughter and tears were shed, all around people were shaking hands and hugging.

The following morning as if by magic thirty eight 4x4 vehicles arrived and transferred us all back to the airport, this time I had a direct flight to Milan and a four hour wait for the flight to take me back to Heathrow. Then a short wait and up the M1 by bus. I was home just before midnight and had a proper cup of tea and then went to bed to bring all the memories back.

The aims of the organizers–Zitoway, were to provide a challenging, but achievable insight into the world of endurance desert running, catering for the relatively newcomer to this extreme race, but tough enough to challenge the more experienced desert racer. They gave us all the ingredients to mix and provided the unique opportunity to fulfil our dreams, enabling us to race in uncharted and fascinating landscapes. They lived up to and fulfilled their promise to bring everyone through the finish line. I would like to thank the Italian organisers Zitoway and their staff, for the abundance of great food and hospitality, they were magnificent; the logistics of the entire event was nothing short of brilliant. Nothing was ever too much trouble and there was always a smile to greet you. "Magnifico, thank you".

A special thanks to the doctor and his staff who worked tirelessly, sometimes late into the night, repairing damaged feet and muscles, getting runners ready for the next day's race and they sorted out dehydration issues. I saw people with drips in their arms and covered in space blankets, they also dealt with a heart attack. After nearly a week in the hospital the guy was allowed to travel home to Italy.

A very special thanks to Phin Robinson of Pure Physiotherapy who sorted out a damaged hamstring problem and got me back in action without having to stop my training, about a month before the trip.

The biggest thanks of all goes to Maureen for putting up with my selfish desires, demands and her understanding of my "Boxes to Tick". She has, without any real complaining cleaned and fed me, put up with hours on end of waiting for me to arrive home after long training runs. Only she will really know what it has meant to me.

My target of 12 hours went out of the realms of realism during that first 5km and the toe problem. The race took a total of just over 16 hours and I felt pretty good throughout the race and was pleased with my recovery after each day's event. I had no aches or pains from muscle fatigue; in fact I was running myself into a better fitness. If ever I was in need of inspiration all I had to do was pay a visit to the medical tent to see the other bloodied, bandaged, dazed and dehydrated athletes being patched up, and realise how lucky I was not to have the damage of some of the more unfortunate runners. This would give me inspiration and put me back on track. My Injury was not such a major problem.

To do anything less than your best is to waste one of life's greatest gifts. This has been a great adventure and one that will give me the confidence to take on bigger challenges in the future.

17
The 'hardest thing' and the 'biggest lesson'

Being part of the successful Phoenix Boxing club meant that our fighters were always in great demand to take part in the frequently held boxing events around Yorkshire and beyond. Much before I had time to settle after my first win at Pitsmoore working men's club, I was informed of my next fight, in pretty much the same manner as I had been told before. The information from Jack Cox about my next opponent came with a sort of, "We are not going to be able to fix you up with a novice again after winning your first fight on a knock out." I couldn't understand what he meant, as my so called knock out wasn't strictly speaking a knock out, the fight was stopped. But that's the way the fighting system works for matching opponents. It was a T.K.O. [technical knockout].

Two weeks later, we set off from the gym, for Southygreen Workingman's club in Sheffield. Although we were a much smaller team of about six fighters for tonight's venue, the same luxury coach was waiting at the gym to take us in style to the fight. My dad couldn't make it for my second fight due to work, but I felt less on edge, and was glad that I didn't have to make conversation whilst travelling to Sheffield. It was good to be able to get my head around what was about to take place again.

We were greeted at the car park to the club, and this time we had plenty of time to spare as we once again made our entrance. This time I felt more a part of the club and dressed in my first pair of long grey trousers, feeling smart and more grown up. The trousers had been a big surprise for me. I was given this brown paper parcel when I arrived home from school a couple of days before the fight. Mum had to set about altering the length of the legs to make them fit whilst I was in bed that night. I had to promise Mum, after strict instructions to only wear the trousers for special occasions.

I had been promoted to second fight on the bill, but first for the club, which gave me time to settle and get ready at a more leisurely pace, and with more time to soak up the atmosphere of the occasion. Before long Jacky had come to get me ready, and this time giving me pre fight instructions, which was making me more nervous. Why did he need to have to give me help before I get into the ring? What did he know that he wasn't telling me about? I suddenly felt conscious of my legs shaking with worry about who I was about to meet in the ring.

"Let's go," he said as he draped the towel around my neck. It was that long walk again, as we pass the opening pair of young boxers coming back to the dressing rooms. We made our way through the avenue of chairs to the far corner of the ring, up the steps, and then the ritual of Jacky lifting the middle rope for me to enter the ring, and into the Blue corner this time, I would have felt better and more at home, if I had been heading for the Red corner, but we didn't get a choice.

My opponent, who was the local fighter, had not arrived at the ring yet, and seemed to be ages before being announced, which was unnerving. Loud cheers were greeting him as he made his way from his dressing room through the crowd and towards the opposite corner. I was doing my best at this time to appear to everyone in the hall as being calm and cool about all this one-upmanship. I turned to see him for the first time as I sensed his arrival in the ring, and nearly died. Stood opposite me, was my opponent, dressed in a silvery blue hooded dressing gown, with the" Southy Green Boxing Club" embodied in dark blue, on the back, and dancing about like a professional. He was doing all what looked like the right things. His coach removed his dressing gown, revealing his now fully exposed vest which was almost full of badges, without gaps, and seemed to be making the muscles on his arms look like Charles Atlas. "Oh my God!" I felt sure they must have made a big mistake, and brought me out with the wrong opponent, as I searched Jacky's face for an explanation 'Now what!' I thought. They make great targets "I could hear Jacky saying from somewhere that seemed a few miles away in the distance. I felt sick and in a complete vacuum. Lamb to the slaughter came into my mind.

We were summoned to the centre of the ring by the same referee that had officiated at my last fight. I think we went through the same instructions, I honestly don't remember what he said, and I couldn't take my eyes off this collection of championship badges on my opponents vest, and was totally mesmerized. I couldn't remember his name either, only that his first name was Alan, which was the same as one of my brothers.

Seconds out, Round One. The next two minutes were a bit of a daze. I was being hit with everything but the kitchen sink. I couldn't work out why I was unable to deal with him, his punches were coming from every direction but where I expected. He was completely dominating the round, making me feel like I hadn't learned anything about boxing, and just the way he moved made me miss with any punch I tried to deliver. I couldn't work out what was going on, and had a sinking feeling, knowing I was losing badly. "How many hands does he have?" The bell was a very welcoming sound, as I made my way back to my corner, bewildered and in a complete daze.

Jacky was already in the ring, and waiting for me. He almost picked me up off my feet as he spun me round, sitting me down onto the stool in the corner, throwing a spongfull of water into my face, almost before I had time to settle on the stool. I had never heard him raise his voice before tonight, but the way he was now delivering instructions at me, really shocked me into complete attention. "He's a Southpaw, so we deal with him by sending him in the opposite direction. Use your right hand. Right hand," he kept saying, and start pushing him round anti-clockwise. "Forget about boxing him, we are going to fight him; we have got to attack. Go for him and get on top. Right hand. Get your Right hand working." So that's what's different, and why I couldn't work out what was happening to me. I had never sparred with, or been taught how to fight a left hander; they are so very different, and difficult to deal with, not just the way they stand, but also the way they fight. I was making it easy for him. Fortunately for me I was able to take most of his body shots without much trouble.

Round two started pretty much like the first, with him on top and punching where and when he wanted, until about half a minute into the round I gave myself a proper talking too, as I realize I was getting slaughtered, it's time to follow advice and get on with turning things around. I set about using the hammered out instructions I had been given, by delivering the best right hander that I had produced to date. My opponent was shocked at the new approach from me, especially as I was now attacking for all I was worth, and at last starting to make him retreat in an anti-clockwise motion. It was his turn to feel the pressure of my new approach, as I started slowly to get on top and dominate the fight for the first time. I had reverted to my early scrapping style, and connecting with some good left and right punches.

Jacky met me coming back to my corner after the second round, with the stool ready set up. He turned me onto the seat, throwing another sponge-full of water into my face, and set about delivering with a sort of excitement in his voice, almost the same instructions as the previous round. Right hand, and attack, was what he wanted, and to keep sending him around anti-clockwise. I was ready to get on with it, well before time was called and eager to make a start on the final round. I really did feel better and had been more in control of the fight for most of that round and certainly better than I had been in the disastrous first round. The second round had been a success for me, and I realised that I had probably learned the biggest fighting lesson of my career to date. I was so glad Jacky Pearson was in my corner.

Round three stared out with a sort of battle for control of the centre of the ring, and one that I was now more determined to power my way into winning. It probably wasn't pretty to watch I feel, as my boxing skills were put to one side, and the scrappy fighter in me took over again. I could tell that he was as much upset by my fighting, rather than the boxing approach, as I had been in the first round with his Southpaw style. I took a few straight jabs to get at him, and within range of him. Determination slowly brought the rewards, as towards the middle of the round I was again beginning to get right on top of this Yorkshire and Northern Counties schoolboy champion. I was now landing good right hand punches almost at will, and pushing him around the ring. Oh what a difference a round has made. Just the look in his eyes, the bewilderment of having to back pedal for most of the round, and not being able to cope with my aggressive style, he probably wasn't used to anyone coming at him like that. I realised that my level of fitness was also a massive help and what made the difference was knowing what to do and having the strength, and stamina to carry it out. I was feeling good at the way I was powering my way on top, as he was now showing classic signs of fatigue, increasingly less able to move as quickly as in the first round. He was reacting much slower and making the targets easier for me to connect with.

The biggest smile I have seen for a long time was on Jacky's face, as I walked across to him at the end of the round. "What have you learned tonight." "To listen" I said. "Yes but what else, badges mean nothing in future," he said, answering his own question and winked at me saying, "you've won this one." I couldn't tell to be honest, but I did feel a lot of satisfaction knowing that I had at least given as good as I had got, and probably more.

Of all the fights that I have been through, this was one that I would dearly have loved to be able to watch over again on video, but of course in those days even a camera would have been something of a bonus. The best we could have mustered up would have been a boxed brownie I think.

The referee who had not had a great deal to do at all during the fight, congratulated us both on a good fight, as he brought us together in the middle of the ring, and this time holding onto my right hand, waited for the judges to come to a decision. I was willing him to lift up my hand as the compare for the evening announced the result. Even when my hand was lifted, and my name was called out, I could hardly believe that I had actually beaten this champion boxer. All I wanted to do was get out of the ring fast, and before anyone could change their minds, but the ritual of shaking hands with my opponent's trainer, and corner men, had to be done. We left the ring together but from opposite corners, and my opponent had to wait for me to make my way to the prize table. Once again I had first choice of prizes. I can't quite remember the choice, but I came home with a very heavy cut glass salad bowl, with two large silver serving spoons. My mum will love this, I thought and she did.

What an incredible feeling, walking back to the changing room, through the isle of spectators, as they stood, sort of hovering over me, and making it feel almost like a tunnel. Most of them wanted to pat me on my back, and shouts of well done, and congratulations were coming from the local crowd. Southygreen workingmen's club would prove to be another place that would become a popular venue for me over the next few years.

A big cheer greeted me, from my club mates, as I walked through the dressing room door. They all wanted to talk at the same time, congratulating me. Jacky took over removing my gloves and hand bandages. We had time to fully discuss the fight round by round, reiterating on the points that had turned the fight around for me. I could see the genuine pleasure on his face, and could feel this new warmth in his voice, as we bonded during those fifteen minutes or so, before he was needed for the next of our club fighters. I now felt towards Jacky Pearson, as I had with Benny Kemp, comfortable and secure, knowing that I was in good hands. I felt that he knew and understood 'Me', I had this powerful glowing feeling deep inside my chest. That unique moment was all too soon interrupted, as Jacky left with his next protégé and our second of the team fighters. At last the dressing room quietened down, and the crowd disappeared to watch the next bout. It was time for me to come down to earth, and absorb the lessons of the day, in peace and quiet, storing these experiences for future use, because I know that is the way forward and the only way to fulfil my dreams.

We fought as a club on a very regular basis in those days, both locally and as far afield as Liverpool, Leeds, and Nottingham, sometimes twice a week, but in general at least twice a month. The Phoenix Boxing club was always in big demand, with a reputation second to none in the Amateur boxing world, and much before I knew it, I was reaching my fiftieth bout without a defeat. It's another milestone in my life that became an unforgettable experience and one that I reflect upon from time to time.

We were fighting at a colliery club in Leicester, and I was matched with one of their British coal board champions. I had no fear in those days whoever I was matched with and when I look back now on those days my attitude had become complacent to say the least. I was un- beatable, invincible.

This part of the story is so difficult to put down on paper, and write about, but is probably one of the biggest life changing experiences, and lessons of my whole life, and needs to be told. So here goes.

We travelled to Leicester on a freezing cold evening, in our usual luxurious coach. I was billed to fight somewhere in the middle of the evening. The ritual of doctor's inspection, warming up and getting ready, was all taken care of without anything unusual happening. I was of course pretty excited, and conscious that this fight would be a special occasion for me being the fiftieth fight.

The fight started, and right from go I was surprised at the inexperience of my opponent. He looked awkward and clumsy. Not what I had come to expect over the last dozen or so fights, it was not a very good match. I genuinely believed that this lad should never be in the ring fighting me, he wasn't ready. I decided to play about with him, and then knock him out in the last round. How facetious is that? That thought has haunted me many times over the years, who did I think I was, as I invited, and even allowed him to hit me, riding the punches to take out the power, as I set about playing with him, making him miss when I wanted, and not really laying a glove on him throughout that first round.

I got a real telling off as I sat down on the stool at the end of the first round. "What the hell are you playing at, let's get on with it". Round two was pretty much the same, and went according to 'my' plans. It didn't matter; I would be knocking him out in the last round. Jacky went absolutely berserk at the end of the second round. He really did blow his top, and came out with a mouthful of real abuse at me, for the first time ever. "You have lost this if you don't knock him out now."

The bell rang for the third round. I set about carrying out my plans, and almost met him coming off his stool. I could see the amazement in his eyes as I hailed punch after punch, looking for his chin; he covered up and backed away. This was now becoming the most frustrating round I had ever fought. I chased him round the ring, throwing punches like a madman trying to land the one that would fulfil my plan of knocking him out. He ducked and dived for the next two minutes, unable to throw a punch at me and somehow avoided any full-on contact from me. The referee stopped the fight a couple of times to wipe his gloves after his back peddling at speed causing him to trip, and go down. Each time wasting precious seconds, that I couldn't use to get at him. The bell sounded far too soon for me, and the fight was over. I was numb inside, and realised that I had just made the biggest mistake of my life. Maybe I had done enough to have won the fight I thought, as I walking back to my corner. The look on Jacky's face told me all I needed to know. He was speechless as he unlaced, and took off my gloves. Less than a minute later, the referee raised my opponent's hand, instead of mine for the first time ever. I had to force myself to shake his hand, knowing full well that I had given him this fight on a plate, and was mad at myself, not at him.

I wanted the ground to open up and swallow me, as I went through all the pent up emotions in my mind. I knew full well that I could blame no one but myself for having violated the spirit of what I had been taught over the last eighteen months or so. The self inflicted punishment that I would put myself through would be nowhere near enough to mend the wrong I had done. It would take a long time for me to feel good again, if ever.

Jacky steered me to one side after we had left the ring and calmly, but sternly told me to take a couple of weeks off, and then come back to the gym and apologise to the whole team and himself for the attitude, and poor sportsmanship I had shown tonight. I had more than deserved this comment, and felt so ashamed of myself. How could I have been so disrespectful, so self-centred, so full of my own importance, so big headed, so full of myself … I could go on? I realise now that this moment had been coming for some time. I had become something of a celebrity over those last few months. Press coverage, and comments that took me from being just an amateur boxer to a great prospect for the future. But these are just excuses for the real reason, I had lost sight of one of the most precious lesson I had learned during my time with Benny and in turn Jacky 'Respect'.

I went through all the emotions of remorse, sorrow and humility over the next couple of weeks, as I tried to come to terms with what had happened to me. Looking back on the next couple of weeks, which were the unhappiest of my life, I went to bed almost every night close to, or in tears. I just wanted to die. Fortunately I was not challenged at school during those days, so I didn't come close to releasing the pent up emotions on any of my school mates.

Entering through the gym doors for the first time after the event was quite traumatic for me. I nearly didn't make it, knowing what was waiting for me, but hoping that the incident of two weeks ago would have dissipated and forgotten about. I nearly turned back. Jacky spotted me as I opened and walked in through the doors. It seemed the whole gym had anticipated what was about to happen as he came over to me, taking my training kit bag out of my hands. "Quiet" "QUIET" he shouted, at the top of his voice, after getting through the ropes and into the ring clearing out two lads, who had been sparing. The room seemed to be closing in on me as I was invited to join him in the centre of the ring. Jacky outlined the chain of events during my farcical fight of two weeks ago, and invited me to comment, and then left the ring, leaving me feeling totally on my own and oh so small and vulnerable. I had been working on a speech that I should make, but couldn't remember a word. The hall became deathly silent, as I stood there feeling small and so insignificant. All the eyes of my team mates, and everyone else inside the hall seemed to be looking right through me as they waited for me to start.

"I am so sorry for letting you all down. I am so sorry for letting the club down, and not doing my best." I was stuttering, stammering, and gasping for breath, as I humbled myself in front of my team mates for what seemed an eternity. Standing inside a ring that had suddenly changed from a place of joy for me, to a sort of dock, with a jury waiting to sentence me to whatever fate was about to be delivered. In the end I just stood there, and had run out of my voice, no sound would come out of my mouth. My heart was pounding in my ears, and I couldn't stop the tears coming, as they streamed down my face. Jacky appeared at the side of the ring after what seemed like an eternity, footed the bottom rope and held up the middle for me to come out of the ring. He never took his eyes off me as he steered me, one arm around my shoulders, towards the dressing room, and away from my staring team mates. As we entered the dressing room, he turned me to face him, and looked directly into my eyes "That took some guts, I am proud of you," and gave me a tight squeeze. "You will never forget this, and that's the last you will hear about it from me he said, but we are going on from here onto better things," he said. Tears were flowing again with relief and the realisation that I was forgiven; I was still a part of the Phoenix boxing club. I had envisaged being kicked out of the club after letting them down so badly. "Swill your face, and get yourself off home. See you Thursday," he said giving me that all knowing wink I was so used to.

Boxing had provided me with an almost showbiz type arena in which to perform, and provided me with a massive buzz. The ring became a stage, which, when I look back on, was my platform for entertaining the crowds. I had lost the fear of competing, but never the excitement. No sooner had I finished one fight, and then I would be looking forward to the next, sometimes even before I had left the ring. My training was so intense at this time, on the lines of a very professional program. In fact Professional fighters were encouraged to visit, and train at the gym, giving me a constant stream of well above amateur sparing, and training methods. I was now able to fight flat out for the three rounds without tiring.

I have a certain type of empathy, and understanding now, when I hear or read about some professional athlete, footballer, or boxer who have gone off the rails, so to speak, and stepped outside the realms of what is expected of them. The press and media create this almost believable situation, where what is said or written becomes believable to the star. There should be a school or college for educating future stars on how to separate reality from fiction. I learned the hard way, and early in my life.

The 'Hardest Thing' I have done in my life, and the 'Biggest Lesson' I have ever learned in my life, all happened before I had reached the age of thirteen, and as it happens both to do with boxing, but the script, as it unfolded, could have been written to encounter any sport, and become life's guidelines. Throughout my life I will never forget these massive influences and what they have provided me with. Unfortunately both Benny and Jacky have passed away, but whilst I am alive they will never die. They are still with me when I most need them. Jacky was right we did go on to bigger and better things over the next few years. But that's another story.

18
Homeward bound

John, my friend who had met me the previous night was here again to greet me at Woodsetts. Did I fancy his company for a couple more of the legs, he asked me. "Great if you fancy more walking now, than running" was my answer. My legs were feeling the miles that had been covered, and needed to be encouraged to perform again as we set off on this leg of the event. Fuelled up with water and more food for me to have on the way, we set off across the playing field and headed for Langold Lakes. It was strange having company for the first time, and I realised that we were now travelling at a faster pace than previously. I was also feeling better with fewer aches than previously as my legs kicked into action again. We soon began to catch and pass athletes ahead of us, who had passed me some hours ago. It was a great feeling as they congratulated me on my double lap, and wished me luck. I mentioned the episode with the fox to John as we passed the lake and headed off towards the woods at Langold; he was impressed with my calmness dealing with the wild ferocious animal.

Catching another group of four athletes we were able to guide them on the route through the woods at Langold. This part of the route was difficult to navigate if you were not familiar with the area, and has caused many a runner to add on an extra few miles in the past. There was no sign of Mr Fox, as we headed out through the woods on our way to Firbeck. Crossing the main Dinnington, Oldcoats road, and down the cinder path towards the ford in the bottom, I could see the three big Shire horses in the field to my left as we passed the large steel gate. Now the welcoming site of the Firbeck checkpoint was coming into view as we crossed the ford and up the lane to the working man's club. These six miles or so seemed to have passed exceptionally quickly, and without any athlete coming past me as we reached the warmth of the Firbeck checkpoint. It would be so easy to spend some time resting and recuperating in this comfortable room as we were provided with a hot drink, dried fruit, chocolate biscuits and fruit cake, but I knew it would not be beneficial to stay and get comfortably settled around the food table. I had to be strong minded and not lose sight of the challenge, so we set off swiftly.

We had left the checkpoint within five minutes and set off at a pretty good pace heading out across the open fields to Maltby, with the now visible pit shaft rising into the skyline to our right. John complimented me on the pace we were travelling. We were now able to predict reaching the next check point at Maltby by about six thirty.

By the time we reached Roache Abbey we had caught up with another athlete who was struggling with blisters to his feet, he asked me if he could tag along with us to get him through the tricky areas before we reached the Crags at Maltby, it was good to have company, it also gave me a good dose of inspiration knowing that I was still travelling pretty trouble free after all these miles. Feeling a bit like a tour guide to our new companion, I was able to point out the history about the two kissing gates, situated close to the Abbey, which were erected in honour of our two running club members who had sadly passed away. One, a good friend called Sandra, who very recently had passed away through cancer. The other, Malc, a few years ago had died whilst out on a training run. Each one of them had spent many hours training around this ancient ruin. The Abbey is beautifully set in this valley, and was landscaped by Lancelot Capability Brown in the 18th century to cover over the ruined areas around the Abbey. This setting has provided a much loved training area for us all over the years.

I was due to pass my cottage within about fifteen minutes, and so I rang Maureen to let her know where I was. Maureen and my daughter Karen, (who had come over to take Maureen to a concert in which she was dancing) were waiting to greet me as I passed through the lichen gate at the church; they were surprised and pleased to see that I was not in any pain, or struggling. I was told that I look amazingly fresh, which made me feel great. I knew that it was also a relief for Maureen, as she would be less worried about me experiencing any problems. We spent a couple of minutes with them, and took our leave to make the next checkpoint before it started to get any darker.

We had left the athlete who had come through to Maltby with us as we headed out towards Old Denaby, and our last check point. John had decided that he wanted to come through to the end with me. He was more than welcome. He is great company, and took my mind off the fatigue that was slowly setting in and now coming in waves.

We only spent a moment at the Maltby checkpoint and set off towards the top of Addison road. The village of Micklebring is as quiet tonight, as it was in the early hours of this morning, as we retraced my steps down towards the M18 motorway and over the rickety old style, heading out along the path towards the willow plantation.

It was now getting dark, and from the lights up ahead we could make out a group of people who were having problems deciding on which route to take as we caught up with them. They now became part of our little gang as they latched on behind us, and made our way up and along the top of the ridge, heading out and leaving Hooton Roberts well behind us.

The group were now dropping back, but I was on a mission and increased the pace as I became more confident now with each step, knowing there was only about six miles to go. We were on our own again as we left the group behind. We were soon dropping down the grassy field to our last check point. I was looking forward to meeting up with Ray and Jane Howarth and the group of helpers. Ray had spotted us coming down the field, shouting his greetings, and waving his torch for us to see. As we arrived at the last check point he grabbed hold of me round my waist, lifts me off my feet, and plants a big sloppy kiss on my cheek, congratulating me. The rest of the gang insisted on a hug, so we all ended up in a group hug before letting me go. "You only have just over three miles to go," he kept telling me. "I am going to ring through to the finish and let them know you're on your way" he shouted as we made our way down the well lit road at Old Denaby towards the railway crossings, and canal towpath beyond.

Crossing over the railway and onto the tow path, we were still making good progress, I was now on a high, the fatigue and stiffness had just about left me, it was amazing to think that there was now less than two miles to go. My phone was buzzing, a text message has come through, "Do I fancy Fish and Chips," I couldn't stop laughing and nearly stepped into the canal as I tried to answer Helen, a good friend who would be at the finish to greet me, I still found it difficult to make my phone function whilst jogging, but I did manage a 'No Thanks'. The path along the river seemed shorter than last night, as we came out onto the road, over the railway bridge, down the steps, and headed through the housing estate towards the canal path again. I had a grin as big as a Cheshire cat on my face, knowing I could crawl from here if I had to.

We were now on the approach to the Manvers College; the whole place was lit up in the night sky. I could actually see the finish area. I feel like I am floating, and my feet are not touching the ground, as we followed the set out route that kept us away from the car park and possible moving cars. I could see the finish line and the greeting party of people who were cheering as we approached... I cross the line!!!

IT'S DONE – Well over one hundred miles, I was still feeling half human and it was also less of a problem than I thought it would be, as I was able to bend down to remove my muddy shoes and socks at the entrance to the hall. I was greeted with a very warm welcome from Helen, who had collected and hands me a plate of pie and peas with mint sauce, and a hot cup of tea, just what I need, as I mention the fish and chips she offered to get me. Although I am a bit reluctant to sit down, I feel comfortable and relaxed as I tuck into the pie. The realisation that there are a good few athletes still to come in brings home the sense of achievement being celebrated. The Harriers officials and supporters of the event were clapping and cheering, together with a good deal of hand shaking from the other athletes. I was asked if I would fancy doing a lap of honour. Ah ah, maybe next year.

I was just about picked off my feet, as Brian Harney came across to the table and nearly squeezed the breath out of me, together with a very genuine, emotional congratulation and this coming from a great distance and record breaking runner. I felt very proud to receive this accolade from him.

I was now wanted for photographs and picked out a spot on the back wall, trying to look like an athlete. I was feeling really good now, and not what I had expected at all. I had no pains, just a little stiff, and a blister on my right heel, which had not been a problem since we applied the plaster the night before. I feel incredibly lucky that I had been able to complete this 100 mile race, which has lasted for a total of twenty six hours, without any real problems. I had been able to cope with the distance, both mentally and physically. I was pleased that I did get the food and drink intake just about right, and would be able to apply that knowledge for future events.

Questions have been answered to a degree, I felt confident that I would be capable of achieving, the very long and demanding endurance desert races, that I had been invited to take part in, without fear of running out of energy. I knew that I would have the ability to maintain the strength of mind I would need to overcome fatigue to be able to make it to the end. I had put my body through a massive challenge, and come through with a greater understanding, knowing that I did my best, to achieving some way towards the best that I am or capable of becoming.

It was time to leave the college, say my goodbyes and thanks to everyone who had supported and helped me to achieve my goal. Just the simple task of being able to bend over and fasten my shoe-laces as we left was so satisfying. Only athletes who have experienced that problem after a long run will understand what a major task that can be.

I would like to express a massive "Thank You" to so many of my friends for their help and encouragement, you all helped make this achievement possible. A very special "Thank You" to my granddaughter Holly, John Clarke, Brian Harney, Ray Howarth, and Helen Woodburn, each one of you contributed in a different but very special way.

Epilogue
It really is possible–just get out there and do it!

Every journey no matter how long it may take, and whatever the distance, starts by putting one foot in front of the other. If you have the desire to step outside your comfort zone and take on a challenge that would become a journey into the unknown, or even something that you did when you were younger and fitter, then conditioning your mind will be your first task and activating the inner aggression that will turn dreams and ambitions into energy and reality. Much has been said and written today about the mental attitude required for success in sports. Training the mind in order to reach one's goal is now a major part of the world's leading sports people. Years ago it was not as prominently endorsed or highlighted as it is now. The natural talent of the individual used to be the emphasis, but it is now agreed that pure guts and determination plays a key role in success. We all have the ability to achieve, but we need to learn how to tap into, and activate the most powerful weapon we posses – 'The mind'.

The next steps are to prepare for the physical challenge, which generally starts by taking on bite sized portions rather than the whole loaf and engaging on a programme of training that will set you up for the journey. Embrace what gives you that good feeling, and take it forward into your next training sessions. The link between the mind and body should not be taken for granted, they work in tandem. Make no mistake if the body is feeble the mind will not be strong enough on its own. Strong body–strong mind.

Assuming that you are physically able to take on the challenge, then you must believe in your ability to achieve. We limit our achievements, only by our fear and inability to believe that we can overcome the unknown element of what it will cost to succeed and it's a sad observation to make, but the ridiculous fear of embarrassment often stands in the way of doing so much more with our lives. A good example of this is the feeling, or comment that 'I shouldn't be doing this because of my age.' I feel that as we age, and generally slow down in line with the natural process of degeneration, we assume that others see us as old and incapable of reaching goals that people of mature years wouldn't normally attempt. My concept of Old has changed year on year. I remember when I was young, anyone over twenty was old. Now anyone over ninety is old. The lesson to be learned is that we are only as old as we feel and that can be controlled by our ability to adapt to the ongoing changes our bodies encounter. We therefore have to learn how to overcome these negative thoughts, and convert them into a positive attitude, and mentally focus on fulfilling our ambitions and dreams. The big secret is to fit somewhere in between and mentally become ageless. Even today I am still passing through doors that my old coaches taught me how to open and it's my intentions to pass on the knowledge that I have gained over the years to anyone who is prepared to listen and put in the effort.

I still passionately believe that my boxing training of years ago provided me with the extra fitness and stamina that I can draw upon, and I still use some of the same routines today. As part of my overall training, I use boxing workouts to give me the extra stamina that is needed to maintain my overall fitness level, and for some months now, a group of likeminded gym members have taken up the challenge, and joined in with my training sessions, seeking advice and help to achieving weight loss, increased fitness levels, and generally enjoying our tough, but light-hearted workout. This group of men and woman without exception put their heart and soul into the weekly training routines.

We generally start the weekly routines by splitting the group into teams. They then race as a team over obstacles, and shuttle runs against one another in the main studio which provides a gymnasium floor area of about 15 meters square. The shouting and cheering from each team provides an electric atmosphere, as each team's members are encouraged to perform to their best, with light hearted banter coming from the opposing team, this provides the camaraderie that in turn encourages friendship, but winning is paramount of course. Bodies are in various states of exhaustion at the end of these first sessions, but set the scene for the demanding boxing workout that come afterwards. Instructions of jabs, hooks, uppercuts, knee strikes, burpees, and press ups are delivered from a CD with a background of stirring music from the Rocky films bellowing out from four large speakers set in all four corners of the studio. This stirring music provides an inspirational session of seven three minute rounds, with a one minute rest in-between rounds. I will pick out and individually help as many as I can, to correctly deliver these punches to focus mitts, simulating full on boxing training. I get an enormous sense of satisfaction watching everyone give their all. This in turn gives me a great buzz, and as long as these guys are prepared to put in the efforts, I am happy to give them my time. The feedback I get from this mixed sized and abilities group, bounces back at me and is so rewarding. One by one at the end of the session they will thank me for the day's workout. It's like a shot in the arm feeding me with an adrenalin boost and makes it all worthwhile.

I am passionate about my sport of endurance running; this sport seems to be more established and accessible in the rest of the world than with the general UK athletes. My aim is now to provide the opportunity for more UK athletes to be able to run in some of the most extreme places on the planet, putting some adventure into our lives and provide incredible memories that will last a life time, not just for the experienced, but also those new to ultra distance running. With that in mind I have teamed up with, and become the sole UK representative for Zitoway Sport and Adventure, the Italian organization, who have for a good few years now, provided the perfect opportunity for runners from all over the world to take up the challenges of desert running. They are about to stage the fourteenth edition of the very successful 100km Del Sahara Race. They have got it right, and professionally stage a number of other events across the planes and deserts of African. The 100km Du Senegal, together with the 100km of Namibia are also multi stage races, and cover a multitude of different terrains. You could say, I have "Been there, done that and got the T-shirt," and now I want everyone to have the opportunity to experience the unique challenges the desert brings. These events which started with a small niche of friends in 1998, has grown into a world class, multi stage venue, catering with passion, and safety, for well over 150 athletes at a time. These races, which are perfect for the athlete new to distance running, will bring a challenge that is achievable but equally tough enough to provide lasting memories. "Have the courage, be amazed, and put some adventure into your lives."

For the more experienced athlete, these races will also provide a demanding challenge, not only against the harsh, changing elements and desert terrain, but against athletes from around the world. Flying the flag for the UK will provide the camaraderie and bring out the passion that is second to none in ultra runners. The series of these multi stage events offer a unique opportunity to experience much more than just a race. Uncharted fascinating landscapes, and often wild animals, provide all the ingredients to fulfill our dreams and ambitions.

Of the three main events, the 100km Del Sahara is rightly called a trail running adventure, and is the flagship of all the events. Physical and Psychological adaptations will be necessary, as athletes take on the less than suitable conditions of the desert for running. The heat or wind and weather conditions are harsh and unpredictable, as I have found out, but the aim of the onsite organization is to bring all the athletes through the finish line. They are more than set up to ensure ultimate safety during all these events.

Gym Buddies

What's coming up for me? In the short term, to keep up my level of fitness I have entered a couple of UK marathons, a 20 & 26 mile tough race across the Derbyshire moors and fells. I will be flying out to Venice in October to take part in the 26th edition of the Venice marathon, shortly after the 50 mile Round Rotherham race, but only once around this year.

Long term goals have been set in my mind with me having every intentions of taking on the desert again. The series, "Racing the Planet" is the main event high on the list of races to do at this stage for the coming year. This event is a series of races across all the major deserts in the world, including the Gobi, Sahara, and Atacama, and will also include the last desert, Antarctica. Each race is two hundred and fifty kilometers in length, with a seven day cut off. They will be a challenging test both mentally and physically.

Looks like it's starting to hurt. Well done guys

The preparation of a fifteen page CV is being collated for submission to gain entry into next year's Badwater race in America, which is staged during July every year. This event is recognized as the toughest footrace on the planet, and attracts extreme adventure racers from all over the world. This one hundred and thirty-five mile none stop race starts in Death Valley, at 282 feet below sea level, and continues out to Mount Whitney with a climb of about 8700 feet, in temperatures of up to, and often exceed one hundred and thirty degrees. The event is by invitation only, and convincing the race organizers that I am capable of taking on this challenge will be a challenging task in itself, as the race is generally oversubscribed each year. I know that if I am successful in gaining entry to the Badwater race, I will have to be mentally and physically at my best to complete this extremely demanding race, to become one of the very few athletes that are inducted into the hall of fame as a finisher. I would dearly love to take part, complete the event, then come back and write about the ultimate adventure of a life time, giving all the full gory details. Will this be the final chapter?